Sales Games and Activities for Trainers

Easy-to-Use Games, Activities, and Exercises
To Teach and Learn How to Sell

Sales Games and Activities for Trainers

Easy-to-Use Games, Activities, and Exercises
To Teach and Learn How to Sell

Gary B. Connor
John A. Woods

McGraw-Hill

New York San Francisco Washington, D.C. Auckland Bogotá
Caracas Lisbon London Madrid Mexico City Milan
Montreal New Delhi Paris San Juan Singapore
Sydney Tokyo Toronto

9 10 11 12 13 14 15 MAL/MAL 0 9 8 7 6 5

ISBN: 0-07-O71847-4

The sponsoring editor for this book was Philip Ruppel. It was designed and produced by CWL Publishing Enterprises, Madison, Wisconsin.

Printed and bound by Malloy Lithography, Inc.

McGraw-Hill books are available at special quality discounts to use as premiums and sales promotions, or for use in corporate training programs. For more information, please write to the Director of Special Sales, McGraw-Hill, Professional Publishing, Two Penn Plaza, New York, NY 10121-2298. Or contact your local bookstore.

 This book is printed on recycled acid-free paper containing a minimum of 50 percent deinked fiber.

CONTENTS

CONTENTS BY TOPIC

Time and Organization

Building Relationships

Questioning Techniques

Presentation Techniques

Handling Objections

Attitude

Product Knowledge

Competition

PREFACE

This book of sales games and activities for trainers has been carefully assembled to give you a wide selection of choices for helping people learn how to sell effectively. It emphasizes the sales person's role as a problem solver and partner to customers. It also stresses the value of teamwork and thinking creatively to take full advantage of the company and other resources to fulfill customer needs.

We have developed exercises for nine different sales skill areas:

- **Time and Organization**. Exercises that cover this topic deal with the issues of time management, territory planning, and personal and presentation material organization.

- **Building Relationships**. Building strong relationships both within the company and with customers is a key element of success. It requires sensitivity to the needs and views of others. The exercises that deal with this topic explore how to build, grow, and use relationships to increase sales.

- **Questioning Techniques**. A big differentiator between the average and the best representatives is their ability to ask effective questions to determine the customer's needs and buying habits. These exercises help to develop this critical skill.

- **Presentation Techniques**. Presentations are the key link to bridging a customer's needs with the company's solutions. These exercises will foster the sharing of ideas on how to do this and help representatives improve their skills here.

- **Handling Objections**. It has often been said that the sale doesn't really begin until the customer objects. Handling objections professionally and accurately is the goal of these exercises.

- **Attitude**. Selling is a mental activity. Sales training can be an excellent catalyst for improving morale and helping representatives gain a positive attitude about their ability to successfully serve the needs of their customers. The exercises dealing with attitude help participants better understand how to approach each sales opportunity in a positive manner.

- **Reinforcement Techniques**. Any new skill must be reinforced several times before behavior changes. The exercises in this category are designed to help participants strengthen many different types of skills.

- **Product Knowledge**. These exercises help participants take a look at their present understanding of the organization's products and services and learn new ways to explain their products and help customers see new applications for the organization's offerings.

- **Competition**. What's the competition doing and how can representatives better understand their position versus their competitors? Exercises in this category help representatives answer this question.

Using This Book

Just as in real life, skills gained in one area also apply to other areas. For example, the exercise "Got It? Use It!" is appropriate in the time and organization area and the reinforcement techniques area.

So, rather than arbitrarily organizing the games and exercises in this book into just one category or another, we have first listed them alphabetically in the contents from "Academy Awards" to "A Zoo Full of Questions." We then follow this with "Contents by Topic," in which all the games and exercises related to any particular topic are listed. Finally, each game and exercise includes boxes at the bottom of the first page indicating the skill areas for which it is appropriate.

In selecting games and exercises for use in your program, you may want to look through the table of contents in the area in which you have an interest. Or you may simply want to page through the book and look at the different games and exercises, discovering which ones might work for you.

It's impossible to come up with completely original games and exercises in a book like this. Though all are aimed at selling skills, those who are experienced in using games in other fields will find some familiar items that have been modified and updated in various ways to apply to selling. We wish to acknowledge and thank all those who have been developing such games and exercises over the past several years from which we have gotten ideas.

Finally, we wish to acknowledge Philip Ruppel of McGraw-Hill who originally suggested this book to us and has been very supportive during its development.

ACADEMY AWARDS

Objective

This exercise is an interesting way to wrap up a long training session. It allows everyone to be involved and gives support to the information that has just been covered.

Procedure

1. At the beginning of the last day of class, explain that there will be an awards ceremony at the end of the session. The awards are given out by the "Academy" and not by the instructor.

   Topics could include
   * Best overall performance in a role play.
   * Best demonstration of a _____ product.
   * Best performance in overcoming an objection.
   * Best organization/time management tip.
   * Most outstanding supporting role in a role play (person playing customer).

2. Have them give thought to the various categories and submit a nomination for the participant that has done the best in that area.

3. Compile the results prior to the end of class.

4. Simulate an actual Academy Awards type ceremony with participants giving out the awards, tearing open envelopes, etc.

Discussion Points

* None other than to stress up front that participants should think through what material was covered and why that nominee was the best.

Materials Required

Envelopes and nomination forms

Time Required

Varies depending on number of awards.

THE ACCOUNT ON ZOOORD

Objective

This exercise is designed to get participants to focus on the presentation materials they have at their disposal and creatively share ideas on their use.

Procedure

1. Explain the following to the class.
   "*Our company has just been contacted by aliens from the planet Zooord. They have expressed an interest in our products and would like to see a presentation. At the moment, all of their spacecraft are tied up, but their Bio-transporter is working well. The Bio-transporter will automatically transfer you from earth to Zooord. There is only one problem; you will only be allowed to bring one brochure/demonstration piece with you.*"

2. Have the class reflect on what they would bring with them, why and what they would do with that during the presentation.

Discussion Points

- Discuss how we often overwhelm our customers with material.

- Explain that frequently too much material and information can raise questions in the customer's mind that weren't there in the first place.

Materials Required

None

Time Required

Varies depending on class size.

THE *AMAZING* COACH

Objective

This exercise is useful in two ways. The first is to give the sales representative an appreciation for the challenges their managers face in the coaching process. Second, it is a good opening exercise to use with representatives who will be acting as mentors to newly hired representatives.

Procedure

1. Hand out copies of the maze (see next page).

2. Break the class up into pairs. One person is to take the role of the "Guide," the other the role of "Scribe."

3. The Guide is to stand behind the Scribe and tell him or her where to draw a line to go from outside the maze to the "sale" in the middle. (You can draw whatever is appropriate for your industry in the center box.)

4. The Scribe is to be blindfolded or close his or her eyes.

5. Allow 3 minutes and try to create a great deal of pressure to be the first team to get to the center. This can be done with a prize for the first team or just by announcing the time on a regular basis.

Discussion Points

*   Discuss how the Guide felt. Look for:
    "Frustrated because he or she couldn't keep the line straight."
    "He or she wouldn't do exactly what I said."

*   Ask the Scribe how he or she felt. Look for:
    "I was trying my best."
    "I shouldn't have been yelled at."

*   Discuss the frustrations that managers endure trying to coach sales representatives and tie those remarks back to the comments collected from the discussion.

*   Finally, discuss steps that representatives can take to communicate more openly with their managers.

Materials Required

Copies of the maze

Building Relationships | Questioning Techniques | Attitude | Reinforcement Techniques

Time Required

10 minutes

THE AMAZING COACH

THE AMAZING COACH

Start   Answer Key

"AND THEY DIDN'T EVEN NOTICE"

Objective

Many sales people thrive on recognition. For some this is the primary motivation. **Many** customers expect service "above and beyond" the normal routine of the sale. The delivery of this added service frequently falls on the sales representative's shoulder. **The** customer may or may not express appreciation for the good deed. When the **recognition** isn't there, it can rub the representative the wrong way. This exercise is to make **the** point that "beyond the call of duty" can be a matter of expected routine by some customers.

Procedure

1. Write the following on the flip chart: WHAT HAVE YOU DONE LATELY FOR A CUSTOMER THAT WENT UNRECOGNIZED?

2. Allow a few minutes for the participants to reflect on this. Encourage them to jot down the following:

   - What did they do?

   - What did the customer say/not say?

   - How did they feel about it?

   - How likely will they be to repeat that act?

3. Go around the room and discuss each participant's issue.

Discussion Points

- Discuss that "above and beyond" is becoming the norm as competition increases.

- Explain that more and more, these acts will not be recognized as something **significant** by the customer. In fact, it may become a routine expectation by some.

- Brainstorm ways that exemplary service can be delivered without requiring a lot **of the** sales representative's time.

Materials Required

Flip chart

Time Required

5 minutes per participant

APPROACHING VERTICAL MARKETS

Objectives

This exercise has three objectives:
* To identify participants in a class who have had success in calling on particular markets.
* To uncover which participants feel they need help with various vertical markets.
* To relax the class and foster open communication.

Procedure

1. Post flip chart sheets around the room. There should be one sheet per participant.

2. Break the group into pairs. Try to pair people who aren't familiar with each other or who don't work together on a daily basis.

3. Have participants divide the page into four equal quadrants with one vertical and one horizontal line.

4. One participant is to interview the other and list the following in each of the quadrants:
    * Upper Left: The participant's name, length of time in sales, and tenure with your company.
    * Upper Right: A vertical market that they have done a good job selling to.
    * Lower Left and Lower Right: Draw a picture of two vertical markets that the participant would like to feel more comfortable calling on.

5. Have everyone introduce their partners.

Discussion Points

* Everyone has strengths and developmental needs when it comes to calling on vertical markets.

* Throughout the session seek out those who have had success in a market that is difficult for you. Share your ideas freely.

Note: Following this exercise, you might wish to use the exercise entitled "Sharing The Vertical Market Wealth."

Materials Required

Flip chart pages (one for each participant)
Pens
Masking tape

Time Required

10 minutes per participant

ARCHEOLOGY ONE OH ONE

Objective

To have representatives focus on the way selling has changed in the past decade..

Procedure

NOTE: This exercise is best done when the class is being conducted in the location **where** the representatives normally work.

1. Set up the "Archeology Hunt" by explaining that a civilization of sales represen**tatives** formerly occupied this office. Their selling techniques were very different from **what** customers expect from us today. Although they are now extinct, there are **artifacts** left that will give us clues as to how they sold.

2. Have the class then set off on a "dig" by going through old files, closets, and **offices** looking for anything that would give clues to how things were sold in the past.

    For example:
    * Brochures that push features rather than needs.
    * Trophies awarded to "The Best Closer."
    * Sales contests that awarded "quick sales."

3. Have each person review their "find" and how selling has changed since the ad**vent** of that artifact.

Discussion Points

* Discuss what has changed radically since these items were created.

* Discuss what types of sales are being rewarded today versus years ago.

* Ask why selling has moved away from a presentation type sale to a more consul**tative** approach. Discuss what customers expect out of sales representatives today and **why.**

Materials Required

None

Time Required

Varies depending on the depth of the "dig."

ARE YOU LISTENING TO MY OBJECTION?

Objective

To demonstrate that sometimes we take for granted that what we hear is what the customer actually means.

Procedure

1. Break the class into three teams.

2. Have the first team sing the nursery song "Twinkle, Twinkle, Little Star."

3. Have the second team sing "Bah, Bah, Black Sheep."

4. Have the third team sing the ABC song.

Discussion Points

• Ask the class how long they have known these songs (all their lives).

• Ask how many realize that all three songs are the same tune.

• Discuss how many times we hear the same objection (the "tune") but because the objection is worded differently, we treat it as if it is something entirely new.

• To further illustrate this, go around the room and have each participant give a different way of saying, "It's too expensive."

• Finish by explaining that everyone knows how to handle the price objection. They just need to be able to recognize it in all its forms.

Materials Required

None

Time Required

Approximately 20 minutes

ASSUMED IDENTITY

Objective

To illustrate that many sales representatives prejudge their customers and make assumptions about their buying habits. This is an effective addition to any role playing scenario. In this exercise, at times different customers will take on assumed roles. For example, they might focus on getting the most for their dollar. At other times, they might just play themselves. Based on the name given to the customer, the representative may make false assumptions about that person's buying habits.

Procedure

1. Pair up representatives for the role plays. Have them sit across from each other.

2. Immediately before the role play begins, place one of the name tents (shown below) in front of the customer. In half the role plays the customers should know their role as indicated on the name and play to it. During the other half, the customer should **not** be made aware of their role and play it any way they would like. In the latter, the customer is not to see the name on the tent.

3. Instruct the sales representatives that they are to address the participant by first name only as shown on the name tent. (If the last name is used, the customer's role may be influenced.)

4. Explain that the participant playing the role of customer may or may not know their name.

Discussion Points

• Ask the person playing the role of sales representative if the customer actually responded the way the name implied. Why or why not?

• Identify which customers actually played the role of the person on their name tent and which were just playing themselves.

• Discuss how we often make assumptions about customers that influence the way we sell to them. Explain that this can undermine the sales process because we are not as open to their needs.

Materials Required

Name tents that indicate a customer's buying habits. For example:

I. M. Cheap	No-need Smith	Wannasee Competition
Gimme Discount	Whobe U. References	Wass Innit Fermee

Time Required

No additional time required from the normal amount of time devoted to role plays. Approximately 15 minutes to debrief.

BUILDING CUSTOMER TRUST*

Objective

Successful selling is based on long-term relationships. Trust between the customer and representative is the cornerstone of this relationship. This exercise will help representatives consider those actions that contribute and take away from that trust.

Procedure

1. Have each participant think of a time when they were burned in a transaction either personally or
professionally.

2. Have volunteers discuss their transaction focusing on:
   * What caused the transaction to fall apart.
   * How they felt about the sales person/company prior to the transaction.
   * What the company/sales representative did or didn't do to make the situation right.
   * How they feel today about that organization.

3. List on a flip chart various issues the class can identify within your organization that cause a loss of trust between them and their customers. Select a few and discuss potential solutions to those problems.

4. Hand out multiple copies of the Customer Trust Grid.

5. Have representatives select one or two customers with whom they have had trouble building trust. Allow them time to complete the form and discuss their plans.

Discussion Points

* Discuss how a key element to resolving customer problems is finding out what they see as the solution to rebuilding a relationship. (Many representatives overlook having this type of discussion with their clients.)

* Discuss that successful resolutions include not only actions, but also agreed-upon dates.

Materials Required

Copies of Customer Trust Grid
Flip chart and pens

Time Required

One
hour

*Used with permission from Buyer's Side Selling, The Connor Group, 1995.

Customer Trust Grid

Customer Name: Date:

What does the customer say the problem is?	What does the customer say will make it right?	What actions will you take to address the issue?	When will you and the customer meet again? What will you discuss?

THE CLIENT'S DAY

Objective

To make representatives more aware of their client's needs and circumstances on any given day.

Procedure

1. Brainstorm with members of the class and list everything that a typical client of theirs might do on a typical day.

2. Review the list and rank the items in order starting with those that have the most impact on their personal success and the success of their organizations.

3. Identify the top three business concerns that a client may have on the type of day you've created.

Discussion Points

- Discuss why "seeing sales representatives" may not be high up on the list (or on the list at all).

- Explain that most clients don't see the value of dealing with salespeople until that value can be demonstrated.

- Discuss ways that the representative's value to the customer can be made more visible at the outset and appeal to the client's business concerns.

Materials Required

Flip chart and pens

Time Required

One hour

COMPETITIVE BRAIN DUMP

Objective

This is a variation on a standard brainstorming technique. The goal is to have your representatives share as much information as possible about the advantages of your company's offering over a given competitor's product.

Procedure

1. Break the class into three teams.

2. One person should be the scribe to record the group's thoughts on a flip chart.

3. When signaled to begin, each team member should describe anything he or she knows about a competitor's weakness.

4. The scribe should list each element on the flip chart.

5. At the end of 15 minutes, each team should present its findings to the remainder of the group.

6. Prizes should be awarded to the team with the most items listed about the competitor.

Discussion Points

- Review the various aspects of the competitor's product.

- Discuss how your sales force can position themselves to capitalize on these weaknesses.

Materials Required

Flip charts and pens

Time Required

One hour

A CORPORATE SCAVENGER HUNT

Objective

To sensitize representatives to all of the sources of information they have available (and need) about their inside customers.

Procedure

Note: This exercise works best if the class is being held in your company's headquarters.

1. With the class, develop a list of information about their customers that they need to determine if there exists an application for their products/services. List these on a flip chart. For example, if you were marketing fax machines you might want to determine which departments in a customer's company send the most faxes and why.

2. Break the class into three or four even teams.

3. Explain that the teams have exactly one hour to find out as much information as they can about their customers and list it on their flip charts. The teams can use any tool that they would normally use to find out information about their own customers. Encourage them to physically walk around the office, use the phone, the computer, or check with other colleagues in their company.

4. At the end of the hour, have each team share their information.

5. Reward the team that gathered the most and best information about their customers.

Discussion Points

- Discuss the various methods the teams used to gather the information and the pros and cons of these methods.

- Ask how this exercise was different or similar to how they gather data on a daily basis.

- Have each participant tell about one new idea they learned from the exercise.

Materials Required

Flip chart and pens
Optional: annual reports, financial statements, and, if possible, Internet access

Time Required

Approximately two hours

CREATE A COMPANY

Objective

For those representatives that call on businesses, it is usually critical that they have a good understanding of the customer's *entire* business. This exercise helps them gain an appreciation of the importance of this understanding and what they might be missing if they only deal with one person.

Procedure

Prior To Class

1. In advance of the class determine who your best representatives call upon in their accounts.
   Establish the following about these accounts:
   * Which departments they call on.
   * Who are the decision makers.
   * What are their typical concerns.
   * What are their needs.
   * What are their objectives.
   * What are their objections.

2. From this information, create a "virtual company" by creating three or four departments. Each department should be staffed by an instructor who is given a script developed from the above information. For further realism, it's a good idea to locate each department in a separate room.

3. Develop an appointment schedule for teams of participants who will be calling on these departments. The appointments should be 30 minutes long followed by a 30 minute debriefing time in between the calls.

During The Class

4. Break the class into teams.

5. Each team should be given their appointment schedules.

6. Explain that each team will call on each of the decision makers. The purpose of these calls is to determine that person's needs, potential applications for your product/service, the future direction of the company, and the decision maker's concerns. They have 30 minutes to interview the decision maker. They are NOT to present any solution or product at any time!

7. Between each of the appointments, they are to debrief as a team and come to a consensus about the needs, concerns, and opportunities.

8. At the end of the last appointment, they are to develop a strategy for this account. That strategy should include:
   - Their assessment of the account.
   - What solution will be presented and how.
   - What obstacles they anticipate to completing the sale.

Note: This portion of the exercise is an effective evening activity during a multiple-day course.

9. Each team should present its strategy using either a flip chart or transparencies.

10. You may want to award prizes to the team whose strategy comes closest to what would be expected from the information used to create the virtual company.

Discussion Points

- Ask participants if they typically conduct a needs assessment of this depth. Discuss why and why not.

- Discuss what team members learned from calling with other representatives. (Usually they will have learned new and different questioning techniques.)

- Explain how much more information and additional applications can be uncovered by calling on these multiple decision makers.

Materials Required

The developed case study and any appropriate props.

Transparencies/Flip charts for the team presentations

Time Required

4 to 8 hours depending on the depth of the case study

THE CUSTOMER'S COMPLAINT*

Objective

Find the Hidden Word type puzzles are hardly new. This exercise uses such a puzzle to illustrate the many reasons customers cancel sales and to position you to engage participants in a discussion on post-call follow up.

Procedure

1. Distribute the word chart.

2. Explain that there are eleven phrases embedded in the chart and they have only 5 minutes to find them. (Do not tell them the nature of the phrases.)

3. Allow 5 minutes for completion.

4. Have participants read what they have circled and list the phrases on a flip chart.

Discussion Points

• Discuss the phrases. Bring out that they represent many of the reasons that customers cancel orders.

• For each phrase, discuss and list what participants could do to prevent such complaints from customers.

Materials Required

Copies of puzzle
Flip chart and pens

Time Required

15
minutes

*Used with permission from Buyer's Side Selling, The Connor Group, 1995

FIND THE CUSTOMER COMPLAINTS!

```
A Y R E V I L E D E T A L E B C C O M E
W D E R O N G I S R E T T E L D Q D A C
E T J K L O D A A R W I O J O N U L E I
R Y U F L N B A B T P R M M C R A I P R
G A L D T W A N I M E D O Z U Y V W H P
T G T W Q U I V L S X V T N E N R O Y R
I H O T M L K P L P O I M J G L A C W E
B R W R A A L S I H E L R N K I I Y R T
K G H A W N I C N T O B R K D O T R G T
W E R G M R M A G O D U X A K N G E A E
B N O U I A P U P B Y O N R M K G A M B
C A L L S N O T R E T U R N E D A W O D
N O S A L E S F O L L O W U P C A L L N
T H K N O O T G B A L T I N E E D A A U
P A H V D A R F L I G H M I N T A T B O
P E R E C I V R E S R O O P S P N O R F
N P C J D B A A M R T J U Q B R E N D T
H O L L A C O T O H W W O N K T N D I D
T W I N O T W H A T W A S O R D E R E D
Q E T U O P I Y A D G J L M B C Z E A M
```

FIND THE CUSTOMER COMPLAINTS!

Answer Key

```
A Y R E V I L E D E T A L E B C C O M E
W D E R O N G I S R E T T E L D Q D A C
E T J K L O D A A R W I O J O N U L E I
R Y U F L N B A B T P R M M C R A I P R
G A L D T W A N I M E D O Z U Y V W H P
T G T W Q U I V L S X V T N E N R O Y R
I H O T M L K P L P O I M J G L A C W E
B R W R A A L S I H E L R N K I I Y R T
K G H A W N I C N T O B R K D O T R G T
W E R G M R M A G O D U X A K N G E A E
B N O U I A P U P B Y O N R M K G A M B
C A L L S N O T R E T U R N E D A W O D
N O S A L E S F O L L O W U P C A L L N
T H K N O O T G B A L T I N E E D A A U
P A H V D A R F L I G H M I N T A T B O
P E R E C I V R E S R O O P S P N O R F
N P C J D B A A M R T J U Q B R E N D T
H O L L A C O T O H W W O N K T N D I D
T W I N O T W H A T W A S O R D E R E D
Q E T U O P I Y A D G J L M B C Z E A M
```

THE CUSTOMER'S FOOTPRINTS

Objective

A lot can be determined about how a customer will react to your product and presentation by learning how they made decisions about other purchases. This exercise will help your class develop questions they can ask to dig out that information.

Procedure

1. Explain that customers typically approach every buying decision in the same way. If we can uncover how the customer made other buying decisions, we can structure our sales approach to meet their well-established criteria. For example, if you are selling copiers, you might ask the customer, "I notice you are using XYZ copiers. Why did you purchase those over other models?" The customer's response will tell you a lot about their purchasing decisions.

2. Distribute blank footprints.

3. Ask for a volunteer and have this person stand on one side of the room.

4. Explain that the volunteer must walk across the room to get to the sale. He or she can only walk on the footprints that the customer has left from previous sales. This person has only 15 minutes to reach the other side before the opportunity disappears. To get there, this volunteer needs the help of the other participants in developing questions that explore past buying decisions.

5. Have participants develop questions to ask the customer about other purchases they have made that will help uncover buying habits. Each of these should be written on one of the blank footprints and placed in front of the volunteer. Each footprint with a question helps the volunteer get one step closer to completing the sale. The goal is to come up with enough qustions to help the person successfully get across the the room in the time allotted.

Discussion Points

• After the person has made it across the room, discuss why customers are more open when discussing subjects not related to what you are trying to sell them.

• Discuss what information can be gathered from those discussions and how they can use this to help complete the sale. Have participants share success stories using this technique.

Materials Required

Blank footprints (use the profile of your shoe and make copies)

Time Required

45 minutes

THE CUSTOMER FROM HELL

Objective

Every representative has a customer that has come to be their worst nightmare. This exercise helps uncover why they can become that way and how to turn around those relationships.

Procedure

1. Place all the supplies listed below on a table in the classroom.

2. Have participants take a few minutes and think about all their customers, particularly the worst they have ever had.

3. Direct participants to use any of the supplies to draw a picture of this "nightmare" customer. Encourage them to use multicolored pens, cut outs from the magazines, etc. to make the illustration as interesting as possible.

4. When complete, have each participant explain their customer. Have each participant sign their artwork and post it around the room.

Note: If you are conducting a multiple-day course, this makes an excellent evening project.

Discussion Points

• For each customer, discuss why that customer became that way.

• Ask what could be done to smooth out the relationship between the customer and your company.

• Discuss what can be done proactively to prevent this from happening to other customers.

Materials Required

Flip chart paper and pens
Old magazines, glue, and scissors

Time Required

Set up:15 minutes
Creation of the "artwork": 45 minutes
Discussion: Approximately 5 minutes per participant

A CUSTOMER PANEL

Objective

To bring into the class a real-world perspective from the customer's side of the desk.

Procedure

1. Invite 5 to 7 customers to your training session.

2. Set up a panel discussion with a moderator to lead the discussion and then open the panel up to questions from the class.

3. It is suggested that you have the class prepare the topics they would like to discuss. Additionally, you may wish to prepare the panel members to answer the following questions:

   - What do you typically expect from a vendor?
   - What expectations do you have for the salespeople calling on your firm?
   - How do you prefer your organization to be approached?
   - What are three things that you feel the best salespeople do?
   - What are three things the worst salespeople do?
   - And similar questions particular to your industry.

Discussion Points

Following the Panel Discussion, review the following:

- What surprises you most about your perspective versus that of these customers?
- How has your perspective on customers changed?
- What will you do differently with your accounts as a result of the things you've learned from the panel?

Materials Required

None

Time Required

2 hours

| Time & Organization | Building Relationships | Questioning Techniques | Presentation Techniques | Handling Objections |

43

THE DAM PROSPECTS

Objective

To illustrate visually that representatives and the company must constantly be prospecting to ensure a continuous flow of new customers.

Procedure

1. Draw the illustration from the following page on the flip chart.

2. Explain that keeping a steady flow of potential customers is the key to successful business over the long run. Further explain that it is like the dam shown on the flip chart. The water (potential prospects) flowing into the reservoir is controlled by the representative. The pipe out of the front represents the actual sales.

Discussion Points

• Discuss what can happen if no prospecting occurs for a long period of time. (If the valve feeding the reservoir is closed, and the water level drops below the drain pipe, no more sales flow out.)

• Discuss the impact of prospecting without following-up to develop the leads. (The water runs over the top of the dam and the "customers" are lost.)

• Explore and try to determine what the ideal mix of prospecting, account development, and closing is in your industry.

Materials Required

Flip chart as illustrated on the next page.

Time Required

15 minutes

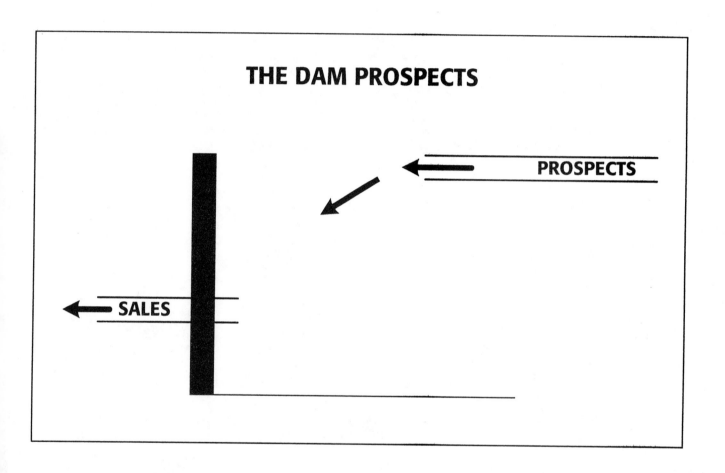

ELECTRONIC NETWORKING

Objective

To reinforce the elements of your program and encourage participants to continue sharing ideas and applications after the class is over.

Procedure

1. Collect and publish everyone's e-mail address during the class.

2. Solicit from the class topics that they would like reinforcement on when they return home. Record on a flip chart.

3. Assign dates to each topic and have participants record those dates in their calendars.

4. Explain that on those dates, everyone is to send an e-mail to the rest of the participants of an idea or success story they have had on that particular topic.

Note: Make certain that as the instructor, you also participate in the exchange.

Discussion Points

*   Discuss why the reinforcement of training is critical to changing behavior over the long term.

*   Ask what they have gained from the interaction with other participants and what benefit it would be to continue that exchange.

*   Get everyone's commitment to this e-mail exchange.

Materials Required

Flip chart and pens

Time Required
30
minutes

FIRST IMPRESSIONS

Objective

To illustrate that not only do customers form first impressions about us, but we do the same about them. That impression can prejudice us in how we approach and deal with that client from then on, sometimes not in our best interest.

Procedure

1. The first day of class, begin the session very low key. Speak in a low voice and in a monotone. Don't smile and limit your expressions.

2. Stop the class. Explain that you are being evaluated by your boss, and she has asked you to have the class write down their impressions of you on an ongoing basis throughout the class.

3. Have participants write down anything that comes to their mind about you.

4. Go around the room, collect the responses but don't do anything with them at that time.

5. Open up and become the real you.

6. Later in the class, have the class repeat the exercise and then compare the comments to the first set.

Discussion Points

*   Why were the participant's initial responses negative? (Your behavior indicated that this would be a dull class.)

*   Ask how many had made up their minds that this was going to be a dull class within the first 3 minutes.

*   Discuss how representatives frequently make the same snap judgments about their customers in about the same time frame.

*   Ask how that kind of prejudice can potentially influence the way respresentatives conduct the sales process, sometimes in ways that can limit their success.

*   Ask how they can be more careful about forming first impressions and to be more open to the differences among their customers and dealing with every person in an effective manner.

Materials Required

Blank sheets of paper

Time Required

Approximately 10 minutes to debrief

FOCUSED ROLE-PLAY CRITIQUING

Objective

When participants are asked to critique role plays, they often focus on the first two or three they see. From that point the attention span wanes and the feedback deteriorates. This exercise is to be used when the instructor sees attention begin to wane.

Procedure

1. Have each participant say on which stage of the sale they feel they are a true expert.

2. Assign the "experts" to each step of the sale so there is a balance.

3. Explain that on the next role play, they are to especially focus on that step of the sale where they are an expert.

4. Conduct the role play but critique by each expert first. ("Approaching" expert critiques first. "Needs Assessment" expert next, etc.)

5. When all of the experts have contributed, open the floor to general comments.

Discussion Points

None other than the above.

Materials Required

None

Time Required

No additional time than that normally allotted for role plays

FORBIDDEN WORDS

Objective

This exercise helps participants change their vocabulary, particularly when you are trying to improve the professionalism of your sales organization.

Procedure

1. Have the class list on the left side of a flip chart terms that they believe take away from the professionalism of selling and imply taking advantage of customers, for example, "Make a deal," "Nail an order," or "Closed 'em."

2. List on the right side acceptable alternatives that imply both sides benefitting from the transaction.

3. Establish that from this point on anyone who uses any of the forbidden terms during the class will have to make a donation to the "class bank." (The bank is usually a jar in the front of the room.)

4. Explain that the class is self monitoring and that they should immediately point out when anyone uses one of the "forbidden words." Also explain that includes you!

Note: It is best to let the class decide what the donation amount should be and what should be done with the "bank account" at the conclusion of the class—distributed to the class members, donated to charity, etc.

Discussion Points

*   Explain that to be professional, we have to speak in terms that respect the customer and enhance our image. This is also an attitude that will lead to long-term relationships and the trust that builds higher sales.

*   At the conclusion of the class, ask how difficult was it to not use the "forbidden words" during the early part of the session.

*   Ask why it is easier to do now. (Practice!)

Materials Required

Flip chart

Time Required

15 Minutes

THE GAME OF OVERCOMING OBJECTIONS

Objective

To give participants practice in handling routine objections that occur throughout the sales process.

Procedure

1. Post the prepared flip charts around the room. Put the game board page on a table in the front of the room.

2. Have participants write on the flip charts the most common objections they hear from their customers about that particular aspect of the sale. (For example, Approaching: "We really aren't interested in your service." Product: "That feature probably won't work here." Hesitation: "Let me think it over."

3. Break the group into three teams.

4. Explain the following:
   - The objective is to go around the board as often as possible.
   - The team will receive 1 million dollars for each time they complete a cycle.
   - The first team to win 3 million dollars is the winner.

5. Process:
   - Each team rolls the single die to determine who goes first. (Highest number, first.)
   - Beginning in the block marked START, the first team rolls the die and moves forward on the board to the appropriate block.
   - They then must respond to the first objection on the matching flip chart page.
   - If they come up with an acceptable answer, they get to stay on that block. If they do not answer to the satisfaction of the instructor, they return to their previous position.
   - Repeat the process for all teams.
   - When all the objections are used up for a given block on the board, that block should be considered "free parking," and those that land on that space should roll again.

Discussion Points

- Ask how many had difficulty dealing with those objections prior to the exercise.

- Ask how the participant's comfort levels had changed.

- Explain that the format for handling objections remains the same no matter where the objection falls in the sales cycle.

Materials Required

Marker pens for each participant

Flip Charts
One sheet each with the following titles at the top:
- Approaching
- Unperceived Need
- Product/Service #1*
- Product/Service #2*
- Price
- Delivery
- Closing

*These sheets will be used for objections specific to a given product or service your company offers.

The game sheet should appear as follows reproduced on the flip chart page:

UNPERCEIVED NEED	PRODUCT/ SERVICE #1	PRODUCT/ SERVICE #2
APPROACH	⟳	PRICE
START HERE	CLOSING	HESITATION

Time Required

Varies depending on the number of objections listed in each block

GOOD AT/NEED HELP WITH

Objective

To develop a network of resources within the classroom.

Procedure

1. Seat the class in a U shape.

2. Give each participant an 11" x 17" piece of paper with the words "Here's What I'm Good At" on the top and "Here's What I Need Help With" about halfway down the page.

3. Each participant is to fill out both sections of the sheet.

4. Go around the room and have each participant review their needs and strengths.

5. When each person has finished, tape their sheet to the table in front of them.

Discussion Points

- *Everyone* has both strengths and developmental needs. No one is strong in everything.

- One of your weaknesses may be a strength of another member in the class and vice versa.

- Encourage participants to come into the middle of the U shape during breaks and seek out those participants who have expertise in their developmental areas.

Materials Required

11" x 17" sheets printed with the words "Here's What I'm Good At" on the top and "Here's What I Need Help With" about halfway down the page.

Time Required

3 minutes per participant

GOT IT? USE IT!

Objective

Throughout training sessions, sales representatives pick up a lot of good ideas that will specifically benefit them in a particular account. Frequently this information is never applied because it has been lost in the shuffle with all the other course materials. This section is a simple-to-use exercise to keep that information intact.

Procedure

1. In the beginning of class distribute copies of the ideas form shown on the next page.

2. Explain that throughout the session, each participant will pick up some great ideas that they can use with specific customers.

3. Participants can use this form to capture these ideas in a structured way so they can use it in the future.

4. As an optional exercise, you may wish to use this as a review form at the end of the class.

Note: Make certain that you set aside time throughout the course for participants to reflect on what they have learned and record those thoughts on the form.

Discussion Points

None other than listed above.

Materials Required

Copies of the Idea Applications form

Time Required

10 minutes to discuss and administer

IDEA APPLICATIONS
Don't lose those great ideas!

IDEA	CUSTOMER TO WHOM IT APPLIES	POSSIBLE OBSTACLES	HOW I WILL OVERCOME OBSTACLES

HANDLING APPROACHING OBJECTIONS

Objective

To help participants work through the most common objections heard from a customer when a representative is trying to approach a new account.

Procedure

1. Go around the room and have each participant reveal an objection they find difficult to overcome when first approaching a new prospect. List as many as possible on a flip chart.

2. When the list is finished, break the class into groups and assign three objections to each group.

3. Each group is given 15 minutes to develop a response to each objection. If they can develop more than one, so much the better.

4. A group spokesperson should review their responses to the entire class and add any suggestions the remainder of the class might have.

5. The list should be typed up and distributed.

Discussion Points

*   Ask how many of the group had difficulty with these objections prior to the exercise.

*   Ask how many now feel comfortable answering them.

*   Reinforce to the class that they, not you, developed the responses.

*   Explain that collective thinking can help overcome many obstacles such as these difficult objections.

Materials Required

Flip charts and pens

Time Required

30 minutes

Handling
Objections

HANDLING OBJECTIONS SHOWDOWN

Objective

Give the class a fun way to practice handling objections.

Procedure

1. Have the class create a list of the most common objections they hear on a day-to-day basis. List them on an easel and number them 1 to 12. (If you have more than 12, start at 1a, 2a, 3a, etc.)

2. Separate the class into teams of 4 to 6. Have each team select a spokesperson and a gunslinger.

3. Give each gunslinger a dart gun and have them approach the target. The first is to take aim and shoot at the target. Note the number of the box where the dart sticks and give that team the corresponding objection from the easel.

4. The team is then given 1 minute to decide on an appropriate response. Only the spokesperson is to give the response. If the instructor decides to accept the response, the team gets one point. If the response is not acceptable, each of the other teams gets a point.

5. As an objection is resolved, draw an X through the box on the target. (If you have more than 12 objections, leave the box open.)

6. If a gunslinger misses the target or hits a box with an X in it, the turn goes to the next team. (Note, you may have to move the gunslingers closer to the target as more objections are chosen.)

Discussion Points

- Ask how many found the objections difficult to handle when they were initially listed.

- Ask them about their comfort level now in dealing with those objections. Make the point that the class resolved each of the objections with no help from you. This will build their confidence in being able to deal with common objections.

- Discuss the value of the teams in coming up with solutions and how discussing sales problems with their peers can be very effective.

Materials Required

Toy dart guns (darts should be the type with rubber suction cups on the end)
Flip chart
Target shown on the next page drawn on a flip chart or a white board (white board is best)

1	2	3
4	5	6
7	8	9
10	11	12

Time Required

Approximately one hour

HELP FOR THE PLATEAUED REP

Objective

There are times when we have to conduct classes for those representatives who have reached a performance plateau. Many of these representatives were very successful at one point. Sometimes that success has been their down fall as management assumed they knew what they were doing and didn't bother with further development. This exercise is designed to have these representatives bridge their past to the future.

Procedure

1. Explain that everyone in the class has a great deal of experience and we want to capitalize on that. Stress that there will be a great deal of sharing in this session and that participants should contribute as much as they take.

2. Distribute the questionnaire and have them complete it.

3. Have the participants share their strengths and what they would like to gain from the class.

4. List on the flip chart their expectations for the class.

5. At the conclusion of the class review the expectations list again. If any have not been met, meet individually with the participant and determine a plan of action to meet their needs.

Discussion Points

- Discuss why we tend to stop doing things that work. (Complacency, short cutting, etc.)

- Reinforce that solid skills never go away, they just need to be tuned up periodically to keep them sharp.

Materials Required

Flip chart page and pens
Copies of questionnaire

Time Required

Beginning of class: 20 minutes (May vary depending on class size)
End of class: 20 minutes (May vary depending on class size)

Where Ya Been?

This questionnaire is designed to stimulate your thinking about your past, current situation and contributions you can make to this class. It will also help clarify what you would like to accomplish in this training session.

Describe the most successful sale you ever made. Why was it successful? What did you do to make it happen?

Complete the following sentence: *I used to be more successful than I am today because*

List 3 things you no longer do that used to work. *(Be honest now!)*

List why you stopped doing those things.

Complete the following sentences:
Here's what I do really well today:

I will be more successful tomorrow than today if I can improve the following skills as a result of this session:

A HELPFUL COACH

Objective

This exercise illustrates that there are two major dynamics going on in any sales process: (1) what is happening in the sales representative's mind, and (2) what is happening in the customer's mind. This exercise is most effective when coupled with an extensive role play and is designed to sharpen the observation skills of all the participants, not just those doing the role play.

Procedure

1. Break the class into role-play teams. Select someone to play the role of sales representative and of customer.

2. Now divide the rest of the observers into two coaching groups. One group will act as a coach for the representative, the other for the customer.

3. Start the role play but stop it at five minute intervals for a huddle. At that time, both the customer and the rep must meet with their coaching team for three minutes to get direction on the next steps of the sale.

4. Continue until the conclusion of the role play.

5. Rotate roles until everyone has been on both coaching teams.

Discussion Points

• Discuss the similarities between what the coaching groups discussed and what we say to ourselves as the sales process goes on.

• Discuss what was helpful/distracting about the coaches.

• Discuss how the customer coaches felt being on the other side of the selling table.

• Stress that coaching help is always available from their manager or other representatives. All they have to do is ask.

Materials Required

None

Time Required

Allow additional time to your normal role play schedule.

HOW POSITIVE ARE YOU?*

Objective

Every day sales are lost because of a sales representative's negativism. What they say to themselves can bring down their attitudes and influence a customer. This exercise will bring some light to how we view neutral events and make them either positive or negative.

Procedure

1. Have each participant take out a sheet of paper and listen to the following story: *Yesterday you noticed water dripping from a pipe under your sink. This morning the plumber arrived right before you left for work. He was to repair the sink and leave the bill. When you arrived at the office there was a message to call the plumber at your home.*

2. Have each participant write down what their self talk is like at that very moment. When complete have participants share their thoughts.

3. On a flip chart make two columns. Don't label them but any time a negative response is made, make a slash in the left column; if positive, make a slash in the right column.

4. When the last comment is discussed, label the columns.

Discussion Points

- Discuss why we tend to immediately think towards the negative in many situations. (Plumbing is typically expensive and not a pleasant experience.)

- Bring out the point that we can choose how we react to any situation and although plumbing is typically negative, selling doesn't have to be.

- Discuss how this negative thinking can come through to customers and influence our sales.

Materials Required

Flip charts and pens

Time Required

15 minutes

*Used with permission from Buyer's Side Selling, The Connor Group, 1995

Building Relationships

75

"I GOT IT, I GOT IT"

Objective

This is a useful tool for the instructor to determine when a class has grasped a given concept. It is also effective in wrapping up a class at the end of the day by allowing participants to recap the key ideas they learned during the session.

Procedure

1. Begin by asking what happens when a fly ball is hit between two outfielders. (Typically one yells "I got it!")

2. Distribute copies of the ball (see next page).

3. Explain that whenever a participant grasps a new idea thoughout the class, they can hold up the ball and say "I got it!"

Note: As the instructor, you may find that you may be able to move through material more quickly. As you cover material, the number of balls held up will give you an indication of what the class is grasping and how quickly.

As an additional exercise, you may wish to wrap up a class day by having participants write the key ideas they got "on the ball" that day. Debrief by going around the room and discussing each ball.

Discussion Points

- Discuss why it was helpful to hold up the ball when they grasped a new concept. (They could see the progress of the class and help those falling behind.)

- If the ball is used as a debriefing exercise, ask how many ideas they heard from others that they had forgotten already.

Materials Required

Copies of the ball (see next page)

Time Required

Varies depending on group size and material covered.

I KNOW WHAT YOU NEED

Objective

To help sales representatives understand the importance of questioning and having an open dialog with their customers before making conclusions about their needs.

Procedure

1. Divide the group into pairs.

2. Have one person in each pair write down a one paragraph description of an animal. This is just a description—do not give the name of the animal.

3. Now each of the writers give their description to their partners. The partner's task is to draw the animal according to this description.

4. When complete, have them share their drawings and see how close they came to the animal the other person had in mind.

5. Reverse the roles and repeat except this time allow the individuals doing the drawings to tell their partners doing the describing what information they need to know to complete the drawing properly (for example: number of legs, what it's covered with—fur, scales, or skin, and so on).

Discussion Points

• How close were the first drawings to the descriptions? What about the second set?

• Why is the second set usually more accurate?

• What does this tell you about listening to customers describe their needs before giving them what you *think* they need?

Materials Required

Paper and pens or pencils

Time Required

15-20 minutes

I'LL BUILD ON THAT

Objective

To help representatives see potential applications they might be missing with an account and develop further benefits they can present when discussing the features.

Procedure

1. Have each participant bring with them a customer profile that includes most of the information your industry requires to determine applications of your product or service.

2. Each round begins by having a volunteer tell the class about their account.

3. When finished, the class is allowed to ask any questions they feel will bring forward additional information not mentioned by the volunteer.

4. Randomly select a participant and have them start by giving what product they would recommend as the minimum solution to this customer's needs and why. For example, "I'd recommend the Model 101 copier because space is limited."

5. Have the person next to that participant tell what they would possibly add to that sale and why. For example, "I'd add the two-sided copying feature to save them paper."

6. The next person should add to that, for example, "I'd add a sorter to save them time collating."

7. Continue around the room until the application is logically exploited.

Discussion Points

- Ask the class if they picked up some new applications for their products.

- Discuss how easy or difficult it was to always mention benefits when discussing features.

- Ask the person whose account was discussed if they found they needed to go back and uncover additional information about the account.

Materials Required

None

Time Required

Varies depending on number of participants. Usually 10 minutes per participant.

I'LL STICK WITH THAT!

Objective

To give representatives a unique way of recording ideas they don't want to lose. To provide an unusual reminder of behaviors participants want to change when they return to the job.

Procedure

1. Hand out "sticks" to each participant.

2. Explain that throughout the course, they should record on the paper any:
   - Behavior they want to change back on the job.
   - New idea they want to implement.
   - Skill they want to further develop.

3. Do not explain why the paper is nailed to a stick at this time.

4. At the conclusion of the course, have participants share what they have written down on the sheets.

5. As an option approximately one month after the course, you may want to mail each participant a twig with a note asking them if they are "sticking" with the skills they learned in your session.

Discussion Point

- Explain that many good ideas and intentions in the classroom are lost back on the job. This unusual method of capturing ideas will help them stick with the concepts when they return home.

Materials Required

Cut tree branches that are approximately 1 1/2 inch diameter into 12" lengths. Nail or staple 8½ x 11 sheets of paper to the stick.

Time Required

Approximately 5 minutes to introduce
Approximately 5 minutes per participant to debrief

INFORMATION OVERFLOW

Objective

This exercise will highlight how representatives frequently over present to their customers, giving them more information than they need.

Procedure

1. Give the class a short scenario that is typical of one of your customers.

2. Explain that each of them is to come up with what they feel is a unique aspect of your product or service that would appeal to this customer.

3. As each person gives you a feature, pour a little water from the pitcher into the glass. Continue to do so even though the glass is full and overflowing.

Discussion Points

• Ask the class why they didn't stop giving you features and benefits even after the glass was full and overflowing. Look for "You didn't tell us to stop."

• Discuss how we have to carefully match our presentations to our customers' needs so that we don't "over fill" them with information that will be wasted.

• You may also wish to make the point that customers may be too polite to let you know they have seen enough. Just as you were too polite to tell them to cease giving you features even though the glass was overflowing.

Materials Required

Pitcher with water
Glass
Towel

Time Required

10 minutes

IT COULD ALWAYS BE WORSE...

Objective

This exercise is good when the class gets bogged down in discussion about a product or service that they think is inferior to the competition.

Procedure

1. Have the participants stand up.

2. Go around the room and have each participant complete the following sentence: "It could always be worse, I could be selling _____." (Suggestions: Carbon Paper, Slide Rulers, Nehru jackets, Telephone dials.)

Discussion Points

• Ask why these things would be worse than the particular product/service they were bashing. (Look for: Market disappeared, Technology changed).

• Ask what they think the sales representatives who used to sell these did when the product became obsolete? (Found alternate markets, sold other products in their line, etc.)

• Ask the class for suggestions on how the class will overcome the shortcomings of the product/service being discussed.

Materials Required

None

Time Required

20 minutes

IT'S A TIE GAME

Objective

To quickly demonstrate to the representatives that we can overlook some powerful details when things get too familiar.

Procedure

1. Have the participants stand in a semi-circle with you in the middle.

2. Have everyone look you right in the eye.

3. Ask the male representatives to tell you the color and pattern of the tie they are wearing without breaking eye contact with you. For women representatives, do the same with either earrings or some other piece of jewelry that is out of their direct line of sight.

Discussion Points

• Discuss how many participants were unable to tell you what they were wearing.

• Make the point that sometimes we overlook things that are very familiar. Some of our long time accounts may fall into that category. We have to make certain that we treat our oldest accounts in the same way that we do a new one. We must constantly be on the lookout for changes and new opportunities.

Materials Required

None

Time Required

15 minutes

IT'S A WAR OUT THERE!

Objective

Every sales representative has his or her share of "war stories." These can be helpful if channeled correctly and disruptive if left undirected. This exercise will allow participants to communicate their stories and you to maintain control.

Procedure

1. Explain that you want to encourage the sharing of ideas and keep the class as "real world" as possible. Also acknowledge that everyone has a few war stories to tell.

2. Clarify that you would like people to share those experiences but that class time is limited so some rules have to apply.

3. Post and review the following rules:
   All war stories:
   • Have to have a positive outcome.
   • Must pertain to the topic being discussed.
   • Must refer to the *current* state of business. (No, "In the old days, we...")
   • Must demonstrate creativity and be completely ethical.

4. You may also wish to set a limit of one or two stories per day per person.

5. When someone wishes to contribute, they can only do so by wearing an army helmet. This will help you control those who wish to monopolize the class with their stories.

Discussion Points

• Everyone can contribute positively, but we have to maximize the impact of every story. That can only be done with a degree of structure.

Materials Required

Flip chart and pens
An army helmet (or a hat of some sort)

Time Required

10 minutes to review the rules

IT'S YOUR COMPANY

Objective

At times a class can get negative about your company or its products. This exercise is useful in getting the class to realize how fortunate they really are.

Procedure

1. Explain that the class has just been given venture capital to start a business to compete with your company. They have all opted to leave your organization and start from scratch.

2. Brainstorm as a group (or break into teams if the class is large) all of the things that will have to be purchased to get the organization to the point where the representatives can begin selling. Appoint a scribe and list them on a flip chart. Keep the ideas flowing as quickly as possible. Include both the item and the approximate cost. Total up the costs.

3. Ask the group how long it would be until they would begin to be paid if all of these expenses were taken out of their commissions.

4. Now go back to the list and cross off all of the things that your company supplies to support the selling effort.

Discussion Point

• Discuss how having their own territories is like owning their own business with much of the overhead paid for by your company.

Materials Required

Flip charts and pens

Time Required

30 minutes

JARGON JAMBOREE

Objective

Many industries are laden with jargon. As insiders, we frequently fall into a form of industry shorthand that causes us to speak using this jargon. This is fine except that many representatives use this "short hand" on customers who may or may not understand the terms. This exercise is a fun way to have participants realize how often they actually use that jargon.

Procedure

1. Choose one person as scribe and have participants come up with as many acronyms and jargon that they can think of, with the scribe writing these on a flip chart.

2. Break the class into teams and divide the list evenly across the teams.

3. Each team is to use the words to form one of the following:
   * A single sentence using as many of the acronyms/jargon as possible.
   * A poem using all of the acronyms/jargon.
   * Use the acronyms/jargon as lyrics to a popular song.

4. Have each team perform their work.

Discussion Points

* Discuss how often jargon is used in the company and how that can carry over into conversations with customers.

* Discuss what can happen if the customer doesn't understand the jargon. (Misunderstandings can result; customer may not ask for clarification and feel intimidated.)

* Brainstorm alternatives to the jargon and acronyms.

Materials Required

Flip charts

Time Required

45 minutes

JUST VISITING, THANKS

Objective

This exercise focuses on how representatives manage their time in front of the customer.

Procedure

1. Break the class into two teams. Assign the first team the term "sales call." Assign the other team the term "sales visit."

2. Have each list the characteristics of both. For example, a characteristic of a visit is, "Doesn't have a goal in mind for the call."

3. Have team leaders present the results to the class.

Discussion Points

- Discuss why some representatives make sales visits instead of sales calls. (Typically, this is to avoid conflict or rejection.)

- Reinforce the positives that come out of the discussion the Sales Call team had.

- Discuss what the impacts are on the customers who experience the sales visit. (They feel their time has been wasted. They may be reluctant to see that representative again.)

- Solicit what representatives can do to turn the visits into more productive calls.

Materials Required

Flip charts and pens

Time Required

30 minutes

KINESTHETIC PRODUCT KNOWLEDGE

Objective

To energize a class and demonstrate the various components of a complex piece of equipment or process. The right brainers love this one!

Procedure

1. Give the class an overview of the product you are about to discuss.

2. Have all participants stand up and come to a large open space.

3. Hand out diagrams of the process you are about to cover. For example, if you were training representatives on how copiers work, you might hand out a diagram of the paper flow through the machine.

4. Have each representative become a part of the machine. For example, one representative might become the paper feeder, another the drum, and another an actual piece of paper itself.

5. Tell each representative that they must be able to:
   * Explain to the class what part their function is in the entire machine.
   * Explain why your brand is better than the competition's.
   * Perform the function of that part of the system.

6. Position each person according to the diagram and have each participant tell the class what they do as part of the system. Then "turn on" the machine. In our copier example, the person playing the role of the piece of paper would move from paper feeder to drum to fuser to final paper tray.

Discussion Points

* Ask participants if they feel they have a better understanding of the workings of the system.

* Discuss why they feel they are better able to describe the significant differences of their product over the competition's.

Materials Required

A diagram of the product about to be trained
Any props that participants might use to better illustrate their part of the system

Time Required

Varies depending on the complexity of the system

LEARN FROM THE BEST

Objective

To share with the class "pearls of wisdom" from the most experienced representatives with the entire sales group. This especially benefits new representatives but all can benefit, including those making the contributions as it causes them to reflect on what they do.

Procedure

1. Three weeks prior to class, fax out the "learning from the best" form to regional sales managers.

2. Have the sales managers conduct the interviews and bring the completed forms to the class or meeting.

3. Collect the forms at the beginning of the class or meeting and screen them. (Some of the tactics used by your most seasoned representatives may not be "in sync" with the philosophy of your sales training.)

4. Read several of those to the class at the beginning of each day and immediately following breaks and lunch. This will not only share the information, but also give participants a good reason to return on time.

5. You may want to make this an annual practice and then copy and distribute these ideas to the entire sales organization.

Discussion Points

- Ask why the class felt that this was a good idea and how they feel customers would react. (This helps internalize the concept.)

- Discuss how hard or easy it would be for the participants to implement this idea. If it appears difficult, further lead the discussion around what it would take to overcome the obstacles.

Materials Required

Form shown below

Time Required

Approximately 5 minutes per idea

Product Knowledge

LEARNING FROM THE BEST

To help bring the best ideas to our sales training classes, we ask each participant to collect **three** great ideas from the most successful representatives in your office.

Please make three copies of this form, select three successful representatives in your area and interview them. They should answer at least one of the three questions below (all three would be great though!).

All three copies will be collected at the beginning of class and shared with the entire group.

Sales Manager's Name:

Representative's Name:

Location:

What is the most creative thing that you do to gain a prospective client's attention?

What is the most original way you have of keeping your clients satisfied?

Give an example of the most effective presentation you have ever done.

MAKE A SALE OF NEW SKILLS

Objective

To help representatives decide on what skills they wish to develop during the course, improve interviewing skills, and reinforce the training following the class.

Procedure

PART ONE. The Course Beginning

1. At the beginning of the course, break participants into pairs. One should assume the role of customer, the other, representative.

2. Explain that one of them is a customer who wishes to buy a new set of skills, either to replace the ones he or she has now or to add to their existing set. Those skills will be sold to the customer throughout the course, but first the representative must determine what the customer needs by interviewing him or her.

3. The interview should be conducted just as the representative would normally interview a customer about their needs. Some suggested questions include:

   - *What's not happening now that you'd like to have happen? The customer should be very specific in his or her answer. "Close more orders" is too general and not acceptable.*

   - *How will you apply these new skills?*

   - *What aspect of the sales process will these new skills improve?*

4. The sales representative should write down what the customer would like to order on the form supplied at the end of this section. The customer should keep a copy of the order.

5. When the interview is complete, reverse roles.

6. If appropriate, participants can share their orders.

PART TWO: During the Course

1. As each "customer" picks up the skills they are looking to gain throughout the course, they should check off the "Received" column on the form.

PART THREE: End of the Course

1. At the conclusion of the course, allow customers time to complete the order form. Each customer should write out what benefits they will derive from each new skill they picked up.

2. You may wish to have participants share how effectively their orders were filled.

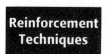
Reinforcement
Techniques

3. Collect, copy, and return the forms to each participant before they leave.

PART FOUR: Post-Course Reinforcement

1. Several weeks following the course, send each participant a bill for the skills they bought during the course. This bill should be the order form with the price section filled out.

2. Payment may be:
    *   Returning a post course evaluation.
    *   A quick note to you as to how they have used the skills.
    *   A quick note as to why they have not used the new skills.

Discussion Points

*   At the beginning of the course, explain that the exercise is to help participants clearly define what it is they are expecting from the class.

*   During the course, periodically sample which orders have been filled to have a sense of whether you are meeting the needs of the class.

*   Prior to the departure of the class, explain the bill and why it should remind them to continually practice their new skills.

Materials Required

Copies of the sales form

Time Required

Part One: 20 minutes
Part Two: Varies
Part Three: 10 to 30 minutes depending on class size and degree of discussion
Part Four: Not applied to class time

ORDER FORM

List the new skills your customer would like to acquire as a part of this course. Do not fill in the "Benefits" or "Date Received" sections until told to do so.

Customer Name:		
New Skill Desired	**Benefits to the Customer**	**Date Received**
	Total Cost:	

MAPPING THE WAY

Objective

Many companies force sales representatives into developing account strategies that fit a specific format. While this may lead to consistency, it can stifle creative approaches to accounts in some representatives. "Mind Mapping" or "Visualization" has been a staple of creative thinking for quite some time. This application of that approach helps many sales representatives break out of conventional thinking and develop more creative approaches to account development. This exercise helps in doing that.

Procedure

1. Distribute a blank flip chart page and pens to each participant.

2. Explain that they are about to begin developing an overall strategy for a large account of theirs.

3. Have participants think through which decision makers or departments they will be contacting. On the flip chart, have them draw a picture that represents that person or department. These should be spaced equal distances apart on the flip chart. The next page shows an example.

4. When complete, have representatives think through what they hope to accomplish with each department/decision maker. That goal should be written next to the appropriate picture. Stress that proper grammar is less important than the free flow of ideas.

5. Now have participants write what the necessary steps will be to accomplish that goal. Again, encourage the free flow of ideas. If participants get stuck on a particular department/decision maker, have them go onto the next.

6. Continue through the process until a solid strategy appears to be developing. As a final exercise, have them explain their strategy to the class and brainstorm alternatives.

Discussion Points

• Discuss why this form of thinking was easier than filling out the typical form.

• Encourage participants to use this method whenever they have to tackle a strategic problem.

Materials Required

Flip charts and pens

Time Required

Varies depending on complexity of accounts

SAMPLE ACCOUNT MAP

Have intro meeting, 6/15

Accounting
Department

*Survey end of quarter
performance, 7/15*

*Spend day observing
exporter, 6/25*

*Meet and discuss past issues
with our company, 6/1*

Sue Jones

*Resolve outstanding
problems, 6/22*

*Schedule meeting,
5/22*

Bill Smith

*Send letter of
introduction, 5/10*

MISSION IMPOSSIBLE

Objective

To foster a sharing of ideas around account penetration. This is also a great exercise to get participants to focus tightly on a single aspect of the sale.

Procedure

1. Have participants write down as much information as they can about an account they are finding difficult to penetrate.

2. Break the class into "Mission Impossible Teams" of four. Explain that in the television show, each member of the team had a specific role and that each person on these teams will have a role as well. Although each person has a role, they are to brainstorm with the team to come up with the best ideas. The roles are:

   • MISSION LEADER: This is the representative who owns the account. He or she should be open to all ideas, record the teams thoughts on a flip chart and finalize an action plan for attacking that account after the class is over.

   • RESEARCHER: Gathered all the background information on the account to be penetrated. They knew where to get the information so that the team knew exactly who to talk to and where to go. On this team, the person playing that role will come up with sources of information to help the "Mission Leader."

   • SAFECRACKER: This person's role will be to develop ideas that will help open the door to the key decision maker. If the recommendation is a letter of introduction or a telephone opening, this person must develop the actual verbiage.

   • ESCAPE ARTIST: This team member must think through all of the things that could go wrong with the plan and lay out a strategy to prevent it. For example, if a screener consistently blocks telephone calls to the decision maker, the Escape Artist has to develop an alternative strategy for getting around that person.

3. Each round should proceed as follows:
   • Each team member takes a role.
   • Mission Leader describes all of the details about the account and answers all questions from the team. They are not to speculate on solutions at this time, just gather information. (10 minutes)
   • Each team member works out a strategy in private. (10 minutes)
   • Beginning with the Researcher, each team member presents their strategy. The team discusses the strategy and possible enhancements/alternatives. The Mission Leader records the output on a flip chart. (20 minutes)
   • When the first round is complete, team members should switch roles so that all have an opportunity to contribute in each role.

Note: If time permits, you may select several Missions and have them presented to the group at large.

Discussion Points

• Discuss what new ideas were gained from the brainstorming. Stress that brainstorming is a very effective way of generating ideas about a tough account.

• Ask if the class feels more confident about attacking those "Impossible Accounts" now.

Materials Required

Flip charts
Optional: Mission Impossible music

Time Required

Approximately 45 minutes per Mission

NAPOLEON'S IDIOT*

Objective

Legend has it that whenever Napoleon would develop a new battle plan with his advisors, he would purposely keep one of his staff membersout of the meetings. That staff member was kept in the dark as to how the plan evolved. Before engaging in that plan the idiot was brought in to look at it from a fresh perspective, unbiased by the deliberations that lead to the plan's creation. This exercise uses an idiot to test out representatives' presentations.

Procedure

1. Break the class into teams and have them develop a presentation about a key feature of one of your products or services. They are to develop this presentation as if they were going to present it to an actual customer complete with presentation materials, etc. Finally, they should develop a list of the 5 key points that the customer should understand at the end of the presentation.

2. Identify several people in your organization that know nothing about the product. Have each team assigned one of these people and deliver their presentation to them.

3. At the conclusion, the idiot should write down what he or she felt were the key points of the presentation.

4. Share the key point list with the team and discuss any gaps or misinterpretations.

Discussion Points

- Discuss why customers don't see all of the key points in the same light we do. Explain how being too close to a product can cause us to assume that the customer knows as much as we do.

- Discuss why some presentations may have communicated more clearly than others.

Materials Required

Presentation support materials
Volunteers to play the role of idiot

Time Required

Varies depending on type of presentations

*Used with permission from Buyer's Side Selling, The Connor Group, 1995.

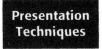

NETWORKING POWER

Objective

To illustrate how effective networking can help sales representatives broaden their sources of references.

Procedure

1. Have participants write down customer references they would like to have. For example, I might be calling on a particular client who has asked me for the name of another customer that uses our products. You may wish to use a reference sheet similar to the one shown on the next page as part of this exercise.

2. The "requests for references" can cover:
   - **Products/Services**: Who else is using your Model M4?
   - **Vertical Market**: Can you give me the names of any other accountants using your service?
   - **Competitive**: Who can I call that has recently switched over from your competitor?

3. Go around the room and have each person ask the rest of the class for references to fulfill one of their requests. Ask the respondents why the references are good.

4. Continue through several rounds if time permits. If not, post the remaining requests on the walls and have the participants fill in referrals during breaks.

Discussion Points

- Discuss why customers ask for referrals; when are they real and when are they merely put offs.

- Ask why references are so powerful and how they should be handled so that the reference is not abused.

- Discuss the power of sharing references and encourage representatives to continue to network within their own sales force.

Materials Required

Optional: you may use either blank sheets of paper or a wanted page (see next page).

Time Required

Varies, but approximately 5 minutes per participant

WANTED

Great References!

I'm looking for a client to whom I can refer my customer for this application:

Suggestions   Your Name

Reward will be paid by:

OFF-THE-WALL APPLICATIONS

Objective

Sales representatives love to tell stories about the most interesting applications customers have found for their products/services. These tales are usually interesting and may actually result in sales for another participant. Unfortunately, we rarely have the time to discuss them at length. This exercise gives a forum for sharing these creative applications.

Procedure

1. On a flip chart draw a cartoon-like picture. (Relax. Any type stick figure will do!) You may wish to tape two pages together for more space. Tape it to a wall in a prominent place in the classroom.

2. Distribute Post-it™ pads.

3. Introduce the drawing to the class as follows:
    "I'd like you all to meet Off-the-Wall. Off-the-Wall has a hobby of collecting the most unusual applications that have been found for our products/services."

4. Go on to explain that throughout the class, everyone is encouraged to write down the most unusual application they have discovered on one of the Post-it™ notes and place it on Off-the-Wall. They are to include their name on the note as well.

5. During the session, participants are encouraged to put up as many notes as possible.

As an optional exercise, have participants vote on the most unusual application of the session. This can be done by having them put a check mark on the note that they feel is the most unique.

Discussion Points

*   Discuss how varied the applications were and how they were discovered.

*   Reinforce that there are many untapped sales in unusual areas if we really seek to find them.

Materials Required

Flip chart drawing
Post-it™ pads

Time Required

Varies depending on class size and number of ideas submitted

OPEN SESAME

Objective

To reinforce the point that open questions can help you gain more information from a customer than closed (Yes/No, Numeric response) questions.

Procedure

1. Tell the class that you are a new customer in their area. The sign on the door only says Ajax, Inc. The office gives no indicators as to what type of business it is.

2. The objective for the class is to determine what kind of business this is and what your needs are relative to his or her product line.

3. Each participant is allowed to ask only one question. After you respond to that question, the next person is to ask his or her question, and so on.

4. When you are asked a closed question, only give limited information. (What kind of computer do you have in your office? An IBX—don't give out the model number.)

5. When you are asked an open question, give out a great deal of information. (Tell me about your computers. We mostly have Panastandard Model 788's. They are about 4 years old and are slower than molasses.)

Discussion Points

* Discuss which questions brought out the most information from the customer.

* Ask why open questions tend to get the customers talking more about themselves.

* Explain that there are times when closed or targeted questions are indeed appropriate and ask the class to give some examples.

Materials Required

None

Time Required

15 minutes

Building Relationships Questioning Techniques Reinforcement Techniques

THE ORANGE TERRITORY

Objective

To illustrate that representatives need to maximize all the potential out of a given territory

Procedure

1. Place an orange on a table in the front of the room.

2. Explain to the class that they are to see this orange as their territory. Further explain that some representatives come into a territory, go for the quick sale and burn the customers in the process. (If you'd like to get flamboyant and smash the orange with a hammer now would be a great time.)

3. Have the class consider how to best stretch the resources of this single orange. (Use the peal to fragrance the room. Squeeze the juice out of it. Eat the pulp.)

4. Make the point that the seeds can be planted to grow even more oranges (referrals and long-range relationships with accounts).

5. Reinforce that like this orange, representatives have to take care of the resources in their territories to maximize their income over a long period of time.

Discussion Point

• Have participants give examples of each point being made above.

Materials Required

An orange

Time Required

15 minutes

Time &
Organization

Building
Relationships

Attitude

ORGANIZING YOURSELF

Objective

To illustrate that without a system for organization, the representative will never be able to accomplish all that is necessary on a given day.

Procedure

1. Fill the bucket with water and place it in the center of the room. (This works best if your room is set up in a U shape.)

2. Go around the room and ask each participant to name one thing that he or she does each day at work.

3. As each person names an activity, drop a ping pong ball into the bucket.

4. Go around the room as often as necessary until the class begins to be repetitive.

5. Ask for a volunteer to come up and hold all of the ping pong balls under water. (One person won't be able to.) Bring up as many volunteers as necessary until all the balls are submerged.

Discussion Points

• Ask why one person couldn't keep all the balls submerged. (Too many of them.)

• Explain that the exercise illustrates that because there are so many things for them to accomplish on a given day, it's vital that they have to have a good system of organization to help them.

• Ask for examples of how different people organize themselves to accomplish all their tasks.

Materials Required

Standard bucket
Approximately 40 ping pong balls

Time Required

15 minutes

PAPERWORK TAG TEAM

Objective

To provide a fun, energizing way to reinforce that paperwork is filled out completely and correctly.

Procedure

1. With an overhead projector, project a blank order form onto either a white board or a flip chart.

2. Break the class into even teams.

3. Explain that each team must fill out the paperwork based on a particular case study that they have just been given. They will be evaluated on the accuracy of the completed form. Each team will start out with a total of 500 points.

4. Have the first team come up to the front and line up in single file with the first person standing approximately 10' away from the board.

5. Hand out the order. At the signal, the first person is to come up and fill in one of the blanks. He or she returns and gives the pen to the next person who fills in the next blank. Continue until the form is complete. Note and record the time taken.

6. Have the other participants evaluate the form and identify any information that may be incorrect or missing. For each omission or error, deduct 10 points from that team's total.

7. Repeat the process with the other teams. Give each team a different order that will require filling out the form differently.

8. Award prizes to the team with the most points.

Discussion Points

- Ask why it was difficult or easy to complete a form in this manner. (Working with others a challenge. The pressure of everyone watching, etc.)

- Discuss why it was easy to critique the other team's orders. Suggest that having someone else review your paperwork is an excellent way to improve your accuracy.

- Discuss why accurate paperwork is important to:
  - The customer.
  - Your company.
  - The representative him/herself.

Materials Required

Case studies based on actual customer orders. These should require the representatives to interpret them and determine what information should appear on the order form.

Overhead projector

Transparency of blank order form

Flip chart or white board

Markers

Time Required

15 minutes per team exercise

15 minutes to debrief

PARTNER OR PLEADER?*

Objective

Many sales tactics of old hardly had the customer's best interests in mind. This exercise will help representatives clarify whether they tend to go for the quick hit orders or form long lasting relationships.

Procedure

1. Discuss what are the classes' perceptions of the terms "Partner" and "Pleader."

2. Explain that this exercise will help them determine where they fall on the continuum.

3. Distribute copies of the Partner or Pleader questionnaire. Have the class complete the exercise. Explain that they are to be completely honest with themselves and that no one will ask where they fall.

4. Score as follows: If the majority of the *even* statements are checked, they are leaning into a Pleading mode of selling. If the majority of the *odd* statements are checked, they are leaning towards the Partner mode.

Discussion Points

*   Discuss the ramifications of Pleading (Loss of credibility with customer. Short-term thinking.)

*   Discuss the benefits of Partnering and what that can mean to your business.

*   Discuss what steps might be taken to move someone from the Pleading stage to the Partnering stage.

Materials Required

Copies of Partner/Pleader handout
Flip chart and pens

Time Required

30 minutes

*Used with permission from Buyer's Side Selling, The Connor Group, 1995

Partner or Pleader?

Place a check next to all the statements that describe something you have done in the last 3 months.

	Check here
1. I have delayed accepting an order to allow the customer to work out implementation details.	
2. I have asked a customer to place an order with us because I needed business in a given quarter or month.	
3. I have asked customers to tell me why they bought a competitor's product or service so that I can learn from the experience, not try to unhook the competition's order.	
4. I dropped my price in order to get a customer to move faster than he or she otherwise would have.	
5. I have put a customer in touch with a competitor if its product better fits the application than mine does.	
6. I have presented my product and price without completely understanding the customer's operation.	
7. I have sent an article to a customer that I thought he or she might find interesting and useful.	
8. I have asked to look at a competitor's pricing or proposal.	
9. I have invited a customer to an industry seminar that I thought he or she might find interesting and useful.	
10. I approach my customers from the standpoint that price is the major focus of their buying criteria.	

THE PERFECT REPRESENTATIVE

Objective

To help participants unleash their creativity and articulate their ideas of the attributes the perfect sales representative should have.

Procedure

1. At the beginning of class, hand out cans of Play-Doh.

2. Explain to the participants that everyone has a mental picture of the perfect sales representative. This is the model that they are striving to be.

3. Have them open the cans of Play-Doh, and make a model of their perfect representative.

4. When complete, have each person describe their model, its attributes, and why they aspire to be like that model. List all attributes on a flip chart.

Discussion Points

• Review all of the attributes and group together those that are similar.

• Ask if some participants in the class already have some of the attributes that are listed. Make the point that we all excel in various areas and also have developmental needs. Suggest that during the class, they try to identify participants who have the skills they lack and spend time picking their brains.

• Discuss ways that participants can learn new skills to become like the Play-Doh models once the session is over.

Materials Required

Play-Doh
Flip chart and pens

Time Required

45 minutes

A PERSONAL COMPANY LOGO

Objective

In many organizations, sales representatives' territories are viewed as their own businesses This exercise helps reinforce this concept as well as foster thinking as to how that "business" should be perceived by customers.

Procedure

1. Explain that representatives should treat their territory like it was their own company. Towards that end, they should think about how they, the company, represent themselves to their clients.

2. To do this, have participants design and draw a company logo for their territories that projects an image of how they would like their customers to think of them.

3. Have each participant explain why their logo looks the way it does.

Discussion Points

• Ask how the logos today are different than they might have been a decade ago.

• Support any indication of customer focus or consultative selling.

Materials Required

Multi-colored pens, magazines, glue, and other art supplies

Time Required

Approximately 30 minutes or assign at the beginning of the class and allow participants to work on their logos throughout the course

THE PICTURE OF ORGANIZATION

Objective

A lack of organization is one of the biggest time wasters that a sales representative can endure. Additionally, sales may actually be lost due to misplaced leads and paperwork. This exercise will help you determine the present state of the organization skill of your participants.

Procedure

1. Distribute the Picture of Organization questionnaire and have participants complete it.

2. Ask how many are closest to the illustration on the left, how many in the middle and how many on the right. (Emphasize that this exercise is not designed to make people feel bad but to help them improve.)

3. Review those habits that participants now have that have contributed to their present situation. List on a flip chart.

4. List what they can do to improve, the obstacles they face, and how they can overcome these obstacles.

Discussion Points

• Ask what are the major benefits that result from improved organizational skills.

• Discuss why we fall into the "disorderly trap" and what steps are required to pull out of it.

• Consider having organized representatives work with those who are less organized to help them improve—maybe set up a buddy system.

Materials Required

Copies of the Picture of Organization handout
Flip charts and pens

Time Required

Approximately 1 hour

The Picture of Organization

Find Yourself on this Continuum

List three habits you have today that get in the way of being organized.

List three habits you have today that contribute to your being well organized.

What are three actions you could take to improve your overall organization?

Obstacles that get in the way of becoming more organized	How I plan to deal with this obstacle

A POSITIVELY NEGATIVE CHARGE

Objective

Customers interpret sales representatives' comments in many ways. We have to make sure that everything we say about our products, services, company, and profession are always positive. This exercise brings to light how we sometimes do speak in negative terms.

Procedure

1. Announce at the beginning of the class that many times we slip into making negative comments about our products, services, or company.

2. Explain that we will be working to change that during this session. Anytime anyone is caught making a negative comment, they will be "fined" a quarter.

3. The class should be self-monitoring and a treasurer elected.

4. At the conclusion of the session, the class should determine where the money should go. Suggestions: Split evenly among participants; Donate to a charity; Hold a drawing, and so on.

Discussion Points

*   Discuss how customers can take comments out of context, particularly if they are negative.

*   Ask for examples of how negative comments in front of customers cost a participant a sale.

Materials Required

A container to hold the quarters.

Time Required

10 minutes to set up the exercise and 15 minutes to debrief.

POST THAT PROBLEM

Objective

Everyone comes to class in search of an answer to some problem or another. In the case of sales training, this is usually focused on a particular account or product/service application. Usually, time doesn't permit discussion of everyone's accounts/problems, but the need is still there. This exercise will allow everyone to get answers and not consume a great deal of class time. (Additionally, over time you will collect data on customer/product trends that may be useful to your organization.)

Procedure

1. Give each participant a sheet of flip chart paper.

2. Explain that we collectively have much more expertise than any individual.

3. Have each participant write on the flip chart a problem they are having with a particular product/service or client. They should also write their name on the chart.

4. Go around the room and have each participant briefly describe their problem. Do not discuss answers at this time.

5. Post the flip chart pages on the walls.

6. Throughout the class, if someone has a useful suggestion for that problem, encourage them to write their thoughts on the appropriate flip chart.

Discussion Points

- At the end of the class, quickly review the information on the flip charts.

- Ask if there are any additional thoughts to add and have the owner of the question write them down.

- Reinforce the power of brainstorming and suggest that they do this often locally.

Materials Required

Flip chart pages and pens

Time Required

Varies depending on size of class

POWER BALANCE

Objective

This is a graphic way to illustrate that the customer doesn't necessarily hold all the power in a buying relationship.

Procedure

1. Have a volunteer come to the front of the room and hold the prepared yardstick in the middle on an outstretched palm so it's balanced.

2. Explain that as representatives, we typically look at the customer as having all the power or "marbles" in any relationship we have with them.

3. Illustrate this by dropping 4 marbles in the cup marked "Customer." (Warn the volunteer so that the yardstick doesn't fall to the floor.)

4. Ask the class what the 4 marbles might represent. (Typically, this will be money, money, and money.)

5. Brainstorm with the class what they bring to the customer that is unique and a benefit. Look for:
   • Industry knowledge.
   • Knowledge of other applications.
   • Information on trends.
   • In-depth product knowledge.

6. For each of these that the class states, drop a marble into the cup marked "Representative."

7. In a short time the balance is restored or may even tip in favor of the "Representative."

Discussion Points

• Discuss why we see the customer as having all the power.

• Explore ways that representatives can demonstrate their expertise in such a way that the customer sees the value they add to his or her organization.

• Have representatives share what they have done to maintain a power balance with their clients.

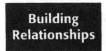

Materials Required

A "balance beam" using a yardstick with two foam coffee cups affixed to each end with tape
Marbles

Time Required

15 minutes

PREPARATION IS THE KEY

Objective

To illustrate how important preparation is to the sales call.

Procedure

1. At the beginning of a day of your class, do the following:
    *   Show up a minute or two late.
    *   Appear to be rushed.
    *   Generally be unprepared. Have some of your materials missing. Make it appear that your overheads are out of order.
    *   Treat the material as if you were "winging" it by asking obvious, rhetorical questions.

2. Continue to play this routine out until the class becomes visibly annoyed.

Discussion Points

*   Ask the class how you appeared to them.

*   Ask how they felt about your ability to meet the needs of the class. (Look for: frustrated, wasting their time, etc.)

*   Discuss how customers must feel when the representative doesn't appear to be prepared.

Materials Required

Whatever you would normally bring into the classroom

Time Required

10 minutes

THE PRICE OBJECTION

Objective

Since the beginning of time, sales representatives have complained that their products have been too expensive. This exercise is designed to illustrate that price is many things to many customers, and that more than price, it is value that is important in the end.

Procedure

1. Have the class think about the last time they bought a car. Ask all how they determined what was a good price for the car.

2. Have the participants write down what price meant to them. List the various meanings on a flip chart.

3. Look for the following:
   * Monthly payments were low.
   * Less expensive than other dealers.
   * Got all the options for the stripped-down price.

4. Discuss how price means many things to people and that price and value are relative to the purchaser.

5. List on a flip chart the different things that "price" would mean to your customers. Further discuss how perceived price can be lowered by adding value or through cost justification.

Discussion Points

* None other than the above.

Materials Required

Flip chart and pens

Time Required

15 minutes

Handling
Objections

PRODUCT KNOWLEDGE OPENER

Objective

While not an exercise per se, this is an interesting way to open a training session on product knowledge.

Procedure

1. Explain to the class that before beginning the section on product knowledge, you would like to read the following excerpt from a corporate message:

   The sales person must become an expert in this line. He/she must be able to advise intelligently every prospect what to buy. To do this he/she must be able to analyze rightly the needs of the prospect and be able to determine the exact needs indicated by this analysis. If after a careful study of the needs of the prospect, the sales representative finds that he/she has nothing that suits this particular case, he/she will refuse to sell the prospect "something just as good," but will advise him where he can get what he needs. Any sales representatives whose work is based upon these high ideals will create for themselves and their organization a confidence and good will on the part of the public that will be a valuable business asset.

2. Ask the class where they think this paragraph originated.

3. Ask the class when they think this reflection on product knowledge was written.

4. Unveil the flip chart to disclose that this was actually written in 1926.

Discussion Points

- Discuss how product and application knowledge along with a desire to help customers solve problems have always been key to the successful sale.

- Discuss how knowledge of the customer's application is as crucial to the sale as is the knowledge of the product.

Materials Required

Flip chart with the following:
From *Keeping the Salesman Fit* by Ben R. Vardaman, Institute of Business Science, 1926

Time Required

5 minutes

QUESTIONS GUARANTEED TO UPSET A CUSTOMER*

Objective

Customers hold a great deal of information that most representatives would love to know if they could only figure out a way to ask. This exercise uses the collective wisdom of the class to bring out the answers to those questions.

Procedure

1. On a flip chart page, prepare the following: "Point Blank Questions I'd Like To Ask But Can't." Some suggestions are:
    "Can you afford this?"
    "Is your credit rating any good?"
    "Are you really the final decision maker in this company"
    Try to come up with other similar questions about information you need to know to successfully complete a sale but can't normally ask directly.

2. Break the class into teams and assign each at least one of the questions. Have them discuss alternative ways to ask these questions or find out this information. Capture this on flip chart pages. When finished, have them tape up their pages on the wall.

3. Have a team leader from each group present their alternative ways of asking for the information or finding out the information.

4. At the conclusion of class have the questions and suggested alternatives typed up and distributed.

Discussion Points

*   Discuss why the "Point Blank" questions would upset customers if asked in that manner. (Questions their integrity for the most part.)

*   Following the last presentation stress that the class developed the correct phrases, not you. Make the point that team brainstorming will always help develop better options than thinking alone and encourage them to do so often with their peers.

Materials Required

Flip charts and pens

Time Required

One hour

*Used with permission from Buyer's Side Selling, The Connor Group, 1995

Building Relationships | Questioning Techniques | Attitude

A QUIETER PLACE

Objective

To illustrate that it is to your advantage to try to move the client into a quiet place that is relatively free of distraction when discussing his or her needs and how you can work together.

Procedure

1. Break the class up into pairs but do not disclose the real reason behind this exercise.

2. Explain that one person is to play the role of customer, the other the role of sales person. The sales person is to interview the customer in the same manner that he or she would conduct any sales call. He or she has 10 minutes to do this.

3. As soon as the discussions start, turn on a tape deck with some loud, upbeat music.

4. Go around to each group and interrupt the discussion to ask any question you'd like. (The purpose is to *interrupt*. The questions you ask are incidental.) Try to get to each pair twice.

5. After ten minutes, turn off the tape deck.

Discussion Points

*   Ask the participants who played the sales role how they felt. (Look for: distracted, had trouble hearing, etc.)

*   Ask the participants who played the customers how they felt. (In most cases, similar to the sales representative.)

*   Make the point that we should try to move the customer to a location where there are few distractions as often as possible. Many reps are reluctant to ask for fear that the customer will respond negatively.

*   Explain that just as in the exercise, customer's find the distractions annoying as well.

*   Ask reps for suggestions and experiences of how they might move a client to a location where they can work together with minimal distractions.

Materials Required

Tape deck and tape of upbeat music

Time Required

15 minutes

Building Relationships | Questioning Techniques | Presentation Techniques

RATE THE PROPOSAL*

Objective

Most major sales involve a proposal at some point. This exercise helps representatives focus in on the key elements of a proposal and how to design them to fit their customer's needs and wishes.

Procedure

1. Prior to the course, have representatives bring examples of proposals that they have delivered or received as customers themselves. At the beginning of the class have each participant choose what he or she considers the best from among those that they brought. Make transparencies of each of these selected proposals.

2. At the session, brainstorm and list on the flip chart what the best proposals should contain. Look for and reinforce the following:
   • Informative but not overwhelming
   • Clear and concise
   • Topics, bullet points and headers
   • Details from a customer's focus

3. Display each of the proposals on a transparency. Have the class consider how well the proposal fits the criteria for the designation of best.

4. Finally, have each participant rate the proposal on a 1– 10 scale. Add up the totals, average, and write this number on the proposal.

5. When finished display the proposal that got the best rating, and copy and distribute it for future reference.

Discussion Points

• Discuss how each person's criteria for the best may have differed and why. Transition that to what customer's may expect from a proposal.

• Ask what are the most effective ways to determine what customers want in a proposal from your organization. (Dialog and questioning)

• Discuss what participants will do differently with their future proposals.

Materials Required

Transparencies
Overhead projector
Flip chart and pens

Time Required

45 minutes

*Used with permission from Buyer's Side Selling, The Connor Group, 1995

REFERRALS

Objective

In some sales environments, referrals are a way of life. Sales representatives ask customers for them all the time. In other industries, obtaining referrals is a great idea, but seldom done. This exercise is designed for that latter group to draw awareness of the power of referrals.

Procedure

1. Read the following story to the class:
   You are sitting at home on a Saturday morning. The doorbell rings and you answer the door. Standing there are sales people from the following industries (show flip chart). Whether or not you purchase something from them, they ask you for as many referrals as legitimately possible.

2. Have participants write down the number of people they would give as referrals to each of the sales people.

3. Go around the room and list on the easel. Add all of them up for a total.

Discussion Points

- Discuss how many times our customers will refer us to others if we only ask.

- Explain that even in the most specialized industries, there are always unknown applications; sometimes even with existing customers. All we have to do is ask!

Materials Required

Flip chart with the following sales people listed:
Insurance
Bottled water
Lawn service
PC maintenance
On-site automobile repair
A video of the week club
Home appliances

Time Required

15 Minutes

SEARCHING FOR FACTS IN CYBERLAND

Objective

To make representatives aware of the information available on the Internet that can help them.

Procedure

1. Solicit and list on a flip chart information that would be helpful in:
    *   Predicting industry trends.
    *   Supplying customers with industry information.
    *   Keeping them abreast of competitive activity.

2. Fine tune the list by creating five specific pieces of information that the participants would like to have on each of the three topics.

3. Identify team leaders who are "Internet literate."

4. Break the class up into teams with approximately 4 participants with a team leader.

5. Assign one category to each team. Have them log onto the Internet and use the various available search engines to research the information.

6. At the end of one hour, have the teams create presentations on the information they uncovered.

Discussion Points

*   Ask how many had never been exposed to the Internet prior to this. Discuss their reactions to the information, ease of access, etc.

*   Discuss how the information that was collected could best be used on a regular basis to gain a selling advantage.

*   Make the point that good customer relations are built on the exchange of information. Sending a customer something of interest to them that you acquired on the Internet is a great way to build rapport and stay in touch.

Materials Required

Flip chart and pens
PCs with modems, Internet access programs and phone line link ups.

Time Required

Two hours

SELL LIKE YOUR COMPETITOR

Objective

To give sales representatives a perspective on their competitor's selling environment.

Procedure

1. Distribute any literature you have on your competitor's products. (You may have to do the "What Do You Know" exercise first.)

2. Assign each representative a competitive product.

3. Have each representative create a customer presentation on that product as if they were the competitive sales representative.

4. Each representative presents the competitive product to the class as if they actually were the competitive representative selling against your company.

Discussion Points

• What did you learn about your competitor's product that you didn't know before?

• How has your perspective on how your competitor sells changed?

• What will you do differently to position your presentations to ward off competitive attacks in the future?

Materials Required

Competitive literature
Flip charts/transparencies as necessary

Time Required

15 minutes per presentation

SHARING THE VERTICAL MARKET WEALTH

Objective

To expand and share the knowledge of various vertical markets within the class.

Procedure

1. Identify and list on a flip chart the major vertical markets called on by your organization.

2. During a break, have participants write their names next to **two** of the vertical markets that they have been successful in calling on. (Note: Prior to this exercise, you might wish to use the exercise entitled "Approaching Vertical Markets.")

3. Separate the class into groups by vertical markets.

4. Each team should select a spokesperson and a scribe.

5. Each group is to list:
   • What are the titles of the decision makers they call on.
   • How they approach decision makers in that market.
   • What are the key concerns for those decision makers.
   • How those concerns are addressed by your organization's offerings.

6. Allow 30 minutes for the group discussion.

7. Without presenting, have participants form groups based on the second vertical market they listed.

8. When complete, each spokesperson should present the group's findings.

Discussion Points

• Discuss similarities from vertical market to vertical market relative to:
   – Level of decision maker called on
   – Approaches
   – Concerns and applications

• Discuss why some approaches work better than others in a given market.

• Explain the benefits of calling on high-level decision makers.

Materials Required

Flip charts and pens

Time Required

Allow 15 minutes for each presentation and 1 hour for group discussion

SLAYING THE DRAGON

Objective

Sales representatives are some of the most creative people to be found. The downside of that is that they sometimes use that creativity to make up great excuses for not being successful. These dreamt-up dragons can get in the way of determining the real needs of the class.

Procedure

1. Give each participant an easel sheet and marking pens.

2. Have them close their eyes while you read the following:

    There once was a brave knight named Sellsalot. He was truly a legend in his own mind and the mind of others. Year after year he accumulated victory after victory. Now Sellsalot was on the edge of the Forest of Fortune. He had trained well. His armor of snappy comebacks was ready to deflect the sharpest objections. His sword was made of the finest sales materials in existence. Yet, the Forest of Fortune caused him apprehension. In the forest supposedly resided the Dragon of Defeat. Some say the Dragon was real, others say it exists only in the imagination. Legend has it that the Dragon of Defeat had destroyed other knights by breathing fire phrases at them so long that they began to believe them and died. Phrases like "You're only a short time success story. You can't keep it up forever." "You're not really very good; you just stumble into things." "I can't believe you even attempt to sell; the competition is much better than you." If Sellsalot can slay the Dragon of Defeat, he can make it through the forest and gain his fortune.

3. Still with their eyes closed, have the class visualize their own personal Dragon of Defeat.

4. Now have them open their eyes and draw the Dragon.

5. Have participants share their artwork and descriptions.

As an optional exercise, at the end of the session have participants come up and slay their Dragon as part of a graduation ceremony.

Discussion Points

• Discuss why the Dragons exist (we all naturally have some self-doubts and feelings of uncertainty) and what we can do to overcome them.

• Discuss ideas to prevent future Dragons from materializing.

Materials Required

Flip chart pages and Pens

Time Required

Approximately 30 minutes

SO YOU THINK YOU REALLY KNOW THE PRODUCT!

Objective

This exercise is more of a "Trivial Pursuit" type game designed to illustrate that you can never know too much about a given product.

Procedure

1. Break the class into equal teams. You should have one team for each product/service that you have covered.

2. Each team must develop five obscure questions about the product/service that has been assigned to their team. (For example: "How many disks does it take to load the XYZ software?" "What is the delivery time from the warehouse to XYZ city?")

3. Stress that the teams must be able to prove the correct answer from the product material handed out during the course.

4. Have each team appoint a spokesperson. You will keep score on a flip chart.

5. Explain that this is a closed book session.

6. Each team has the opportunity to ask the other teams one of their questions. The first team to get it right is awarded a point. (Due to the obscure nature of the questions, no points are deducted for a wrong answer.) Should no team get it correct, the point goes to the asking team.

7. When a question is resolved, the next team has the opportunity to ask theirs, and so on.

Discussion Points

• Discuss how many possible aspects there are to all products and that the better we know them, the more comfortable we are in assessing customer needs for a potential fit.

Materials Required

Flip chart and pens

Time Required

One hour

STONES OF THE SALE

Objective

To have representatives maintain their focus on the next step of the sales process rather than just on closing the order. This helps reduce self imposed stress and allows them to think more clearly about what they have to do next.

Procedure

1. Lay the stones face down on the floor (in order) approximately 24" apart.

2. Ask for a volunteer and have him or her stand approximately 24" away from the first stone.

3. Explain that he or she is about to cross a stream and this person must do so by stepping from stone to stone.

4. Have the participant cross the stream by walking on the stones.

5. Ask for a second volunteer. Explain that he or she has to cross the same stream only by focusing on the other shore.

6. Have the volunteer attempt to cross without looking at the stones.

7. Turn over each stone and conduct the discussion below.

Discussion Points

• Ask the class what happened to the second participant when he or she strictly focused on the other shore. (He or she gets wet.)

• Ask the class why the first volunteer made it across dry. (He or she went from stone to stone.)

• Explain that the sales process is a series of steps that they must focus on individually. If representatives only focus on the other shore (closing) they most likely will not think clearly about the next things that they are to do with the customer.

• Additionally, if all they think about is the result of the call, they will put unnecessary pressure on themselves.

Materials Required

Create a series of stones out of construction paper. On one side should be written a step of the sales process (For example, approaching, fact finding, and so on.)

Time Required

Approximately 15 minutes

STOP ME BEFORE I LOSE THE SALE

Objective

To help sales representatives recognize when they are about to lose a sale because they have given the customer too much information.

Procedure

1. You can administer this exercise in one of two ways:

   - Identify two members of the class who are good actors. Have them read the scripts.
     or
   - Make enough copies of the entire script for each member of the group to read individually. They can then indicate where the sale went off track.

2. Tell participants, "We are going to review a sales presentation. Here's what I'd like you to do while you are listening/reading:
   - Take note of what the customer's interests are.
   - Indicate when you feel the sales representative should have stopped the presentation."

Discussion Points

- What are the customer's interests?

- When should the rep have stopped the presentation? Why?

- When did the sales person lose the sale?
  Look for this answer: When the rep began to discuss the speed and handling of the car.

- What does this say about paying attention to customer needs when making a sales presentation?
  Remind the class that this exercise helps us appreciate that what you don't say is as important as what you do say.

Materials Required

Enough copies of the script for everyone if people are reading it or two copies if you do role play

Time Required

30 minutes

Scenario: Auto World

Bill: Good afternoon. Welcome to Auto World!

Miss Boyle: Hello.

Bill: How can I help you?

Miss Boyle: Well, I'm in the market for a new car. The last one I bought in 1984 seems tired, so I thought I'd look around.

Bill: Well, you've come to the right place. Do you mind if I ask you a few questions Miss...

Miss Boyle: My name is Miss Boyle. I'm a retired school teacher.

Bill: Miss Boyle, tell me about the driving you typically do.

Miss Boyle: Mostly just short trips around town. I fly or take the train on longer trips. Those fast cars on the interstates are more than this 68 year old can handle.

Bill: Is it usually just you or are there others with you?

Miss Boyle: Once in a blue moon I'll have my neighbor's little boy with me, but that's pretty rare. For the most part it's just me.

Bill: Miss Boyle, what sorts of things are you looking for in a car?

Miss Boyle: That's a good question. Let's see... It has to be economical. A retired school teacher doesn't have a lot of money, you know. I want something that's small so I can park easily. It doesn't have to go real fast. Oh, I know what I don't want though!

Bill: What's that?

Miss Boyle: I *don't* want a lot of those silly gadgets I see on other people's cars. Honestly, my neighbor Ellen just bought a car with all sorts of nonsense. Buttons to roll up and down the windows, a gadget to open the trunk from inside, reading lights, and even a thing that shows the outside temperature. What a waste of money!

Bill: I suppose that everyone has his or her own likes and dislikes.

Miss Boyle: (Whispering) I think she was swindled by the sales person!

Bill: I see. Do you have any particular color in mind?

Miss Boyle: Anything but red!

Bill: Well Miss Boyle, I think we have the perfect car for you. Let's take a look over here at our newest model, the Lightning.

Miss Boyle: Gee that looks nice. Small, so I can park it, and I like the color.

Bill: The Lightning is one of our best sellers. Most people like it because of it's features and handling. Why don't you have a seat in it?

Miss Boyle: OK. Gee this is nice and compact.

Bill: That's right. The Lightning was built for handling and maneuverability. It's small enough to fit in the tightest spaces.

Miss Boyle: That's what I like. These shopping center parking spaces seem to get smaller all the time.

Bill: I think you'll also find it economical. It gets almost 40 miles to the gallon and doesn't require a tune up until 60,000 miles.

Miss Boyle: 40 miles to the gallon. Imagine that! It's a lot better than that gas guzzler I've got parked out front there.

Bill: The gas mileage comes from the enhanced design of the Hypro engine. It's economical but can also go from 0 to 60 in less than 9 seconds. With its dynamic suspension, you can take some of the tightest turns without any loss of control.

Miss Boyle: I see. Well speed isn't a big thing for me...

Bill: The power braking system with the antilock brakes gives the Lightning one of the shortest stopping distances around. Those brakes combined with the new air bag system, make this one of the safest cars on the road today.

Miss Boyle: As I said, I don't drive real fast so brakes and things like that don't do a lot for me. What is this thing?

Bill: That is one of the best features of the car Miss Boyle. It is a cruise control system that senses hills and even the wind and adjusts the speed of the car automatically for you.

Miss Boyle: You mean I can't control the speed myself?

Bill: Oh sure you can. Most people just use this for long trips.

Miss Boyle: Oh...

Bill: And see that control there? That is the rain sensing wiper control. As soon as it begins to rain, the wipers turn on immediately.

Miss Boyle: Are these fancy systems extras?

Bill: No, they are built into the cost of the car. So are a number of the other standard features like the power steering, AM/FM cassette player, and automatic door locks.

Miss Boyle: I'm not real big on the gadgets. I just like a car that...

Bill: Did you notice the built in cup holders and map light? Those are some of the little extras that come with the Lightning.

Miss Boyle: And probably boost up the price. As I said, I'm looking for something fairly simple.

Bill: The Lightning is one of the best values on the market today. Would you like to test drive it?

Miss Boyle: No, I don't think so. It's probably more than I can afford and besides, all that speed and handling would be wasted on an old lady like me.

TAG TEAM RELAY

Objectives

To help participants learn about complex products
To energize participants
To reinforce product training

Procedure

As an example, we will use a copier to illustrate this exercise. Create similar activities for whatever your product or service is.

1. Break the class into groups of 5.

2. Have as many products at the front of the room as you have teams. (If you have three teams, you will need three copiers.)

3. Assign each person on the tag team a task. For example, the first person must load the paper; the second person makes three copies; the third person makes three two-sided copies; and so on.

4. Line up the teams single file.

5. At your signal, the first person runs to the copier and performs his/her task. They run back and tag the second team member. That person performs his or her task, runs back and tags the next, and so on.

Discussion Points

• How did it feel to be able to perform product routines under pressure?

• How does this relate to how smoothly products should be demonstrated in front of your customers?

• What does this tell you about practicing product demonstrations on a regular basis?

Materials Required

Necessary equipment and supplies
A whistle to begin the race

Time Required

Approximately 30 minutes depending on the complexity of the tasks

10 GREAT THINGS ABOUT A NO*

Objective

In many sales representatives' minds, a "no" is paramount to total failure. If that rejection occurs early enough in a day, it can influence the state of mind for the remainder and jeopardize other sales as well.

Procedure

1. Ask how many participants have heard a "no" in the past week. Discuss the context of the "no."

2. Ask how the participants felt when they heard that and how long they were discouaged as a result. Further discuss how, when they were discouraged, what attitude they may have been presenting to other customers.

3. Break the class into teams. Explain that they have been commissioned to write material for a late night talk show. The producers have just called and said that they need a list entitled "The 10 Best Things About Receiving A No."

4. Allow 10 minutes and then have the class share their lists.

Discussion Points

• Further discuss how important it is not to lose perspective when rejected.

Materials Required

Flip chart and pens
A good sense of humor

Time Required

20 Minutes

*Used with permission from Buyer's Side Selling, The Connor Group, 1995

THEY AIN'T ALL THE SAME AFTER ALL

Objective

To have participants realize that all customers are not the same despite having similar appearances on the surface.

Procedure

1. Break the class into teams of six.

2. Pass out bags of candy to all participants. (M&M's work well for this.)

3. Instruct participants not to open the bag but just examine it on the outside. Ask if all participants have identical bags of candy. (Most will say yes.)

4. Have participants open the bags and dump out the contents. Encourage them to look for differences from bag to bag. (Number of pieces, color combinations, sizes, shapes, etc.) They should discuss this as a group and then share with the class.

Discussion Points

• Discuss the differences from bag to bag. List on the left side of a flip chart.

• Make the point that many customers appear to be the same on the surface, just as the unopened bags did. Using the differences on the flip chart, make linkages to customer needs. Some suggestions include:

Difference	Linkage
Number of pieces that were different.	A business's overall size might appear the same but they may have very different distributions internally (financial, manpower, etc.).
Mix of colors was different.	Applications may vary from business to business. Always keep a look out!
Some bags had more defective pieces than others.	Quality control may vary drastically from client to client.

• Summarize by reinforcing the fact that you can't judge any customer by appearances alone.

Materials Required

Bags/Boxes of candy (M&M's, Good & Plenty, Jujifruit, etc.)

Building Relationships   Questioning Techniques   Presentation Techniques   Product Knowledge

TOMBSTONE TERRITORY

Objective

Many sales representatives are too harsh on themselves over sales that they have lost. This exercise is designed to help them look at a lost sale in terms of a learning experience and to get the negative aspects of it behind them.

Procedure

1. Explain that the class has just entered Tombstone Territory, the territory where all the sales are lost.

2. Either pass out tombstones or have participants use blank sheets of paper.

3. Have participants think about the most recent sale that they lost and why.

4. Each representative is to draw a tombstone for the lost sale and create an epitaph for that sale. (Refer to some of the epitaphs below.)

5. Go around the room and have each person explain what happened and why.

6. Create a grave yard in a corner of the room where all the tombstones are gathered.

7. Throughout the class, as ideas and techniques surface select tombstones that represent sales that would still be alive if the participant knew then what he/she has just learned.

Discussion Points

• Ask how many participants were dragging this tombstone around in their minds by beating themselves up over the loss of the sale.

• Discuss how there is something to be learned from every lost sale. That's how we get better.

• Reinforce the importance of analyzing each sale and growing from the experience.

Materials Required

Blank paper or tombstones as shown

Crayons or markers

Time Required

15 minutes to introduce the exercise and create the tombstones
5 minutes each to debrief

RIP

Smith Company

Ed's objection was strong
He was no fool
I lost the order
Objection not overruled

RIP

Jones Manufacturing

I loved my product
It couldn't be neater
The sale was lost
I only talked features

TRAFFIC COURT

Objective

To provide a fun way of giving balanced feedback to role-play participants.

Procedure

1. Hand out blank tickets to the role-play observers (samples are shown at the end of this section.)

2. Explain that at the conclusion of each role play, they are to give the sales representative two tickets:
    *   A Commendation Ticket for something he or she did well.
    *   A Summons for something that he or she needs to improve on.

3. Explain that they are to fill out not only the type of ticket, but also their reasons for giving it.

4. Encourage the class to use their own creativity, but on the next page are some suggested tickets. (Note: You may wish to copy these to a flip chart and post.)

Discussion Points

*   Discuss why balanced feedback is important to a person's overall development.

*   Ask if receiving feedback in this manner helped the participants to better remember the areas they need to develop and the things they did well.

Materials Required

Copies of both Summons and Commendation Tickets

Time Required

Varies depending on number in class and number of role plays

POTENTIAL SUMMONS

Speeding	Talking too fast for that customer.
Driving on the wrong side of the road	Missing an application or trying to sell something that the customer wasn't interested in
Illegal parking	Dwelling too long on one aspect of a product or service
Failure to yield	Interrupting a customer
Lane change without a signal	Jumped from one topic to another without making sure the customer was following
Hit and run	Closed the order without establishing a followup plan
Driving under the influence	Was all over the place and was difficult to follow. Endangered the sale and those around him/her.

POTENTIAL COMMENDATIONS

Heroism	Facing up to a difficult customer/situation and making the best of it
Outstanding rescue	Recovering a sale from a position where it might be lost
Firefighter	Calming the flames of an upset customer
Pulled from bottom of the well	Took a customer from a position of no interest to a point of purchasing

SUMMONS	**COMMENDATION**
This is to summon_____ to court for the following violation:	To applaud _____ for showing strength, valor, and tenacity in the face of customer adversity, we issue the following commendation:
For the following reason:	For the following reason:
This summons is being issued to help you develop your skills, improve the profession of selling and increase your earnings.	This commendation is being issued to encourage you to continue to develop your skills and do the right things for your customers.
Officer:_____	Officer:_____
Date:_____	Date:_____

WHAT CARTOON ARE YOU?

Objective

This exercise is a visual way to have participants introduce themselves and give you some insight as to their selling style.

Procedure

1. Explain that as part of the introduction the participants must tell about how they see their selling style.

2. To do this, they must select a cartoon character that best mirrors their style. Some examples:
   - Popeye: A strong closer.
   - Mary Worth: A good listener.
   - Dick Tracy: Does a lot of detective work prior to making a call.

3. You may wish to have them write the character's name or draw the picture on their name tent.

Discussion Points

- Discuss how participants had to reflect on their selling styles prior to the selection of a character.

- At the end of the course, ask if participants would choose another character who would better fit the sales representative they would like to be.

Materials Required

None

Time Required

Slightly adds to the normal time for introduction

WHAT COULD POSSIBLY BE WORSE THAN THAT?

Objective

Selling is an emotional business. As a representative, you are always exposed to rejection. That is why positive self talk is a key to staying in the right frame of mind. However, when the pressure is on the representative to produce, negative self talk starts in the minds of many. This exercise is to help bring that negativism out into the open and expose it as being ridiculous.

Procedure

1. Explain that self talk is great when its positive and deadly when it goes negative.

2. Have each participant think through a tough pressure situation when their self talk turned negative.

3. Have them write down what they were saying to themselves when they were really beating up on themselves. (For example, "I'll *never* overcome that objection.")

4. Break the class up into pairs and have one representative read his or her negative self talk to another. When finished the partner is to ask "What could possibly be worse than that?" The rep must then respond. ("I won't hit quota.") Following that, the rep is again asked "What could possibly be worse than that?" ("I'll lose my job.")

5. Continue until the answer is reduced to the ridiculous.

6. Reverse roles and repeat.

Discussion Points

• Ask how many participants routinely have the negative self talk that they wrote down on the paper.

• Discuss the impacts of that kind of thinking on both the rep and his/her perception by the customer.

• Ask how many have actually thought the thoughts that were stated following the question.

• Conclude the discussion by bringing out that negative self talk is harmful but left unchecked can be devastating. Then make the point that the reality of that first negative statement happening is as good as the final, truly ridiculous one.

Materials Required

None

Time Required

30 minutes

WHAT DID YOU LOSE?

Objective

Usually as a wrap-up exercise, trainers ask questions about what the sales representatives *gained* from a class. Participants expect that and give some degree of thought to that question. This exercise will cause them to think deeper and give the trainer a better insight into behavioral change.

Procedure

1. As a wrap up exercise, have participants:
    *   Give thought to their approach to selling prior to your course.
    *   Reflect on what changes they plan on making as a result of the material covered.

2. Now have each participant answer the following question: "As a result of what I have learned in this course I am going to lose _____."
    *   Example: "I am going to lose my fear of cold calling."
    *   "I am going to lose my inability to call on Attorneys."

3. Go around the room and use this as the debriefing exercise.

Discussion Points

*   Conclude the exercise by summarizing any major trends of losses.

*   Encourage participants never again to "look for" or "find" their loss, but rather to focus on their gain.

Materials Required

None

Time Required

Approximately 3 minutes per participant

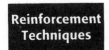
Reinforcement
Techniques

WHAT DID YOU SAY?

Objective

To create an awareness of how often in any interaction we are too busy thinking about what we are going to say next and not focusing on what the customer is saying.

Procedure

1. To start this activity, tell participants that an important part of interaction is simply hearing one another. Hearing does not necessarily mean understanding, however. To demonstrate this, try the following experiment.

2. Have two volunteers come to the front of the room.

3. Their assignment:
   Person 1 is to describe out loud the route of his or her drive to work on a typical morning, street by street. For example, "I backed out of my driveway and went east on Oak Drive, and then..." and so on.

4. Person 2 is to repeat out loud as many thoughts as he or she can remember that were running through his or her mind on the drive to the session that morning. For example, "I started out thinking about how I had to remember to get the Edmonds proposal in the mail before the meeting started. Then I remembered that I had to get gas..." and so on.

5. They are to talk *at the same time* for exactly 3 minutes.

6. The class is to listen to both, but the goal is to try to learn and remember what route person 1 took to work that morning.

7. At the end of the 3 minutes, ask the class to write down what route Person 1 takes to work.

8. When complete, have Person 1 again repeat the description of the drive again and have the class check to see if they got it right.

Discussion Points

• How many of you got the directions right?

• How many found it easy? How many found it difficult?

• Did the chatter of person 2 interfere with your ability to listen to person 1?

• Can you relate this problem caused by person 2 to the mental chatter that often goes on in our minds as we interact with others?

Building Relationships   **Presentation Techniques**   **Reinforcement Techniques**

- What does this tell us about quieting our minds so that we can actually get the message of the person we are conversing with?

- Why do we mentally wander off in front of a customer? Aren't they saying things that we should be paying attention to?

In Participants' responses, look for answers like:
"We think faster than people talk. Thus our minds tend to wander."
"Many reps are so focused on what they are going to say next that they stop listening to the other person."

This exercise demonstrates how listening attentively to everything the customer has to say is vital if you want to actually hear his or her message. The way to deal with this is WILLPOWER. Plain and simple. When you start to wander off, bring yourself back quickly! To avoid the trap of thinking what to say next, make sure you've heard all of what the customer has to say before you decide what to say next.

Materials Required

Paper and pens or pencils for listeners

Time Required

20 minutes

WHAT'S IN THE BRIEFCASE?*

Objective

Many representatives try to plan for every possible contingency when making a call. Often, this manifests itself as an overstuffed briefcase that gives a poor impression to the customer.

Procedure

1. Have each person take out a blank sheet of paper. Listing one item per line, have them write down everything in their briefcase.

2. Separate the class into groups of 4. Tell the class the following:

   "Congratulations! You have just been selected to make your company's first sales call on the only business on the planet Mars. Due to the vast distances involved, we can't tell you anything about this customer other than the call will be like most others you make every day. This will most likely be a one-call sale.

   "We can only carry a limited amount of weight on board the spaceship. Therefore, you will only be permitted to take five business things in your briefcase."

3. Have each team brainstorm the five most critical things needed to make the sales call on Mars. (Assume that all food, clothing and other personal necessities will be supplied. Only those things needed to make the call will be required.)

4. Allow 15 minutes for the exercise then debrief.

NOTE: As an option, you may wish to bring in trash cans and have a briefcase cleaning session.

Discussion Points

• Discuss how our briefcases get to be so cluttered in the first place. Highlight the poor appearance that we give to customers.

• Note the similarities between the groups and discuss the differences.

Materials required

None

Time Required

30 minutes

*Used with permission from Buyer's Side Selling, The Connor Group, 1995

Time & Organization

WHAT'S THE NEWS

Objective

To illustrate that representatives need to keep up to date on current trends that can impact their business.

Procedure

1. Distribute full copies of the daily newspaper.

2. Break the class evenly into groups. Assign each group one of the following:
    *   International news
    *   Business news
    *   Happenings in Washington
    *   Domestic news
    *   Stock market
    Note: You can tailor these topics to better suit your industry.

3. Each group is to review the paper and focus on their assigned area. They are to seek out any news that day that they feel may impact your company or any of your customers. Each group is to find at least three news items.

4. At the end of the "research" have a spokesperson from each group explain the findings.

Discussion Points

*   Ask if any of the class has routinely viewed the daily news in this light.

*   Ask what are the advantages of doing this.

*   Discuss what the class will do with this information, especially how it affects sales opportunities.

*   Discuss what other sources of information should be "mined" on a weekly basis.

Materials Required

Newspapers for each group

Time Required

30 minutes

WHAT'S YOUR GUESS?

Objective

To illustrate that none of us have the same initial perceptions about a given customer and that the perceptions we do have may not be correct.

Procedure

1. Distribute the "What's Your Guess" handout **face down** to all participants.

2. Explain that they are about to meet four customers for the first time. When told to do so, they are to flip the page over and quickly jot down their initial impressions of each of the four people on the page.

3. They are not to discuss their impressions with anyone else in the class.

4. When finished, have them indicate which person is most likely the key decision maker in that organization.

5. Have all participants share their impressions and who they feel is the decision maker. (You may wish to keep score on a flip chart, particularly who is the decision maker.)

Discussion Points

- Discuss why everyone had different impressions of the "neutral people" on the page. (Everyone's background, experiences and perspectives are different.)

- Ask why there was such a disparity in the selection of the decision maker.

- Reinforce the point that everyone is correct. Any of the four could be decision makers and that we can't judge from the initial appearances.

Materials Required

Copies of the "What's Your Guess?" form. (See next page.)

Time Required

Approximately 15 minutes depending on the class size and degree of interaction

Building Relationships   **Questioning Techniques**   **Attitude**

What's Your Guess?

WHY?

Objective

This is a variation on the Repetitive Why type exercise. It is designed to have sales representatives really get into the motives of their customers and have a better understanding of that individual.

Procedure

1. Have the class give some thought to the most difficult customer they have dealt with in the past month. They should particularly think about the customer that most baffled them.

2. Have participants write down the following (see the form on page 211):

   What was the history that led up to that meeting?

   What was going on around that customer when the discussion took place?

   What was the customer's body language?

   What specifically did the customer say?

   What is your best guess as to what was going on?

3. Break the class into pairs.

4. Have one person describe what they listed for items 1 - 5. The second partner is then to challenge the representative's speculation in item 5 by repeatedly asking "Why do you think that is?"

   For example, the discussion might go something like this:
   "He said that he never wanted to deal with us again."
   "Why do you think that is?"
   "He doesn't like us as a vendor."
   "Why do you think that is?"
   "Maybe he isn't comfortable around me."
   "Why do you think that is?"
   "I can be a little aggressive at times and he is on the shy side."

5. The pair should then brainstorm out ways to turn the situation around.

Discussion Points

- Ask if at the end of the discussion, the class had a clearer picture as to the cause of the problems with the customer?

Building Relationships | Handling Objections | Attitude | Reinforcement Techniques

- Discuss some of the situations that turned out not to be at all what they first seemed to be.

- Discuss the benefits of using the repetitive "why" to try to understand the customers point of view.

Materials Required

None

Time Required

Varies depending on class size

Why?

Answer the following questions about your customer as honestly as you can.

Customer's Name:

What was the history that led up to the meeting where you experienced the problem?

What was going on around the customer at the time the discussion took place?

What was the customer's body language?

What specifically did the customer say?

What is your best guess as to what was really going on?

WHY DO BUSINESS WITH US?

Objective

This exercise will help sales representatives realize that their expectations and those of their customers are not always the same.

Procedure

1. Develop a questionnaire for the participant's customers that measures their expectations of your sales force and sales representatives in general. (If this information is available from your normal customer surveys, there is no need to do bullet two.) Questions should include:
   * What are the qualities you expect from our sales representative?
   * How often should you be contacted by our representative?
   * What is the major function you would like our representative to perform between our two organizations?
   * What would you like our representatives **not** to do with your account?

2. Prior to the class, have participants distribute five of the attached questionnaires to their customers. The participants are not to read them, and the customers should be requested to seal them in an envelope.

3. In class, have representatives brainstorm what they feel will be the customers' responses to the questionnaire. Use a separate flip chart page for each question. Record the representatives' responses on the left.

4. Open the envelopes, tally the information and record the customers' remarks on the right column.

5. Compare the similarities and differences.

Discussion Points

* Discuss why some of the customers expectations were higher than participants thought.

* Discuss why some might have actually been lower.

* Brainstorm ways that each participant could meet or exceed those expectations.

Materials Required

Copies of questionnaire
Flip chart and pens

Time Required

Approximately 1 hour

YOU SHOULD HAVE SEEN THIS ONE!

Objective

Sales affords us an interesting perspective. Although we sell everyday, we also *buy* everyday. This gives us an opportunity to professionally observe a number of styles and compare our own abilities to those of others. This exercise is a variation on the standard best/worst listing. It will foster the sharing of some of the best and worst we have all seen.

Procedure

1. Have participants complete the Best Rep/Worst Rep questionnaire.

2. When complete have everyone share their Worst Rep story first. Reinforce what could have been done differently by that representative.

3. Have everyone discuss their Best Rep story. Try to make connections between what that representative did well in his/her business and what could be applied in your own industry.

4. Use this information to lead into your session saying that we hope the skills learned here will keep all of us out of the Worst Rep category.

Discussion Points

- Discuss that there are many things that impact the success and failure of every sales representative. When discussing the worst rep, try to look for the underlying cause of the lack of performance (lack of training, support material, etc.).

- Reinforce the fact that no one wants to do poorly.

Materials Required

Copies of Best Rep/Worst Rep questionnaire

Time Required

Approximately 5 minutes per participant

| Time & Organization | Building Relationships | Questioning Techniques | Presentation Techniques | Handling Objections |

227

You Should Have Seen This One!

Complete the information below about the best and worst sales representatives you have encountered.

Worst Rep

Describe the situation you were in when you encountered this representative.

What specifically did he or she do that made him or her less than effective?

How can you avoid what they did so as not to duplicate their mistakes?

Best Rep

Describe the situation you were in when you encountered this representative.

What specifically did this individual do that made him/her effective?

How can you apply this same skill in your present position?

YOUR COMPANY HISTORY

Objective

Most sales representatives are proud of their organizations and don't hesitate to tell the customer about the corporate history. While most representatives will describe products in terms of benefits to the customer, they may neglect that same approach when discussing the company history. This exercise is designed to make the sales representatives aware of that division.

Procedure

1. Explain that you are about to conduct a company history quiz with a twist.

2. Have everyone write down three pieces of corporate history. For example, "Who founded the company?" "How long in business?" And so on. Explain that these should be things that they routinely tell the customers.

3. Quickly go around the room and have each participant tell his or her three.

4. Now ask the class why a customer would have any interest in those statements as they were just told.

5. Have the participants go back to their statements and revise them with a customer benefit attached to each.

6. Go around the room again and have each participant say them again.

Discussion Points

• Ask how many participants never thought about presenting the company in terms of benefits to the customer.

• Discuss why that may have occurred. (Many think benefit presentations are limited to just product/service.)

Materials Required

None

Time Required

Varies depending on number of teams

A ZOO FULL OF QUESTIONS*

Objective

This warm-up exercise sets the stage for any session that deals with effective questioning techniques.

Procedure

1. Break the group into pairs.

2. Assign the name of an animal in the zoo to each person in the room. They are not to share which animal they have been assigned.

3. Each person must try to determine what animal the other person is by only asking questions that elicit "yes" or "no" responses.

Discussion Points

- When finished, discuss the following:
  What kinds of questions were most productive?
  What kinds of questions led nowhere?

- Explain that in most cases, wider ranging questions provide more information. For example, if you asked "Do you have wings?" that would provide you with limited information and you would have to ask many additional questions to get your answer.

- However, if you asked "Do you live on the water or on land?" a yes or no response would rule out a large number of options and get you needed information more quickly.

Materials Required

None

Time Required

20 minutes

*Used with permission from Buyer's Side Selling, The Connor Group, 1995

About the Authors

Gary B. Connor is the head of The Connor Group. He has developed and sells the sales training program "Buyer's Side Selling." He also delivers seminars and does speaking on sales, sales management, and time management. He is on the Board of Directors of the Professional Society for Sales and Marketing Training and the Board of Directors of Sales and Marketing Executives. Connor lives in Fayetteville, Georgia.

John A. Woods is president of CWL Publishing Enterprises, a firm that specializes in the development of business publications. He is co-editor of McGraw-Hill's *The Quality Yearbook* and *The ASTD Training and Performance Yearbook.* He lives in Madison, Wisconsin.